THE PREDATOR

THE PREDATOR

PAT E. ROBINSON

XULON ELITE

Xulon Press Elite
2301 Lucien Way #415
Maitland, FL 32751
407.339.4217
www.xulonpress.com

Unless otherwise indicated, Scripture quotations taken from the King James
Version (KJV) – *public domain.*

Edited by Xulon Press

Paperback ISBN-13: 978-1-66284-767-7
Hard Cover ISBN-13: 978-1-66284-768-4
Ebook ISBN-13: 978-1-66284-769-1

Endorsements

My friend Pat is dedicated to turning her personal hurts into helping others who have experienced violence. Many other victims look back and see only empty arms, rejection, or unspoken words of love. She has received peace through God's leading. This true story will help many to learn from their past, and to live in their present without being afraid. Pat details resources to help abused victims understand the dismantling equality in the relationship and become survivors.

-A special friend, Betty Weddle

… an encouraging story of faith, perseverance, and determination in times of trial, and a God whose ways may sometimes seem strange, but whose love really does endure forever. I'm sure this book will help God's people 'weep with those who weep' and shine forth the comfort and mercy of Christ Jesus.

-Pastor David Mora

For we preach not ourselves, but Christ Jesus the Lord; and ourselves your servants for Jesus' sake. 2 Corinthians 4:5

I am at your service - God Bless

Pat Robinson and I have been friends for several years and I have actually never know anyone that has had several close calls with death and harassment by such a troubled, sick charming man. Her story touched my heart several years ago and I asked her to speak before my Bible Study telling how God rescued her out of this controlling situation. I know she would not be alive today if she had not placed her trust in Jesus to help save her when she was in the trunk of a car when he was beating her or when she was in chains. Only God was there! I honestly believe she went through this trial in her life to help other ladies, get out, or recognize not everyone that is a charmer is normal.

Ladies her story is real and may we all protect our teen girls and help friends that are in an abusive relationship. If a man disrespects you in any way, RUN before you fall into a TRAP you can't get out of. Pat is now working with the Prosecutor's Sexual Assault Response Team and different agencies to promote domestic violence awareness and to educate violence awareness to educate women as to how they can get help.

Pat is a kind, soft spoken beautiful lady that is also tough. She has a strength and determination to help ALL WOMEN find help so no one will ever be a victim with no one to turn to. I encourage you to read her book so that you may also help yourself, your children and other women. Thank you dear lady for sharing your journey so that other may open their eyes to domestic violence.

Love you friend may God have his hand upon this book to bring him glory and help others to have the courage to speak out.

-Dee Hamond

Pat Robinson has been my neighbor for 25 years. I've known her and her husband Gary as wonderful faith-filled people who have willingly shared their home with family members as well as foreign exchange students. It wasn't until recently that I learned of Pat's survivor details of domestic violence experience which she endured at the hands of an abuser over 30 years ago. The details she shared were shocking and horrendous. After being content confined to a wheelchair from foot surgeries, she worked tirelessly recounting the nightmare into written pages hoping to enlighten others of how the hand of God miraculously freed her from her captor's violence. Pat's passion and courage to share her story inspired me to unlock the secret abuse I endured in my first marriage. It is Pat's hope that she can help victims through domestic violence awareness, education and honesty.

-Cheryl Ballinger

ACKNOWLEDGEMENT

To those who cared

Dedication

My Husband for His Loving Support

In 2003, God sent a loving Christian husband, Gary into my life. He showers me with genuine love and companionship. His support and compassion helped me in my long healing process. His love and prayers supported me as I wrote about the violence and relived it. Gary's encouragement helped me write from my heart and soul. To my loving husband, Gary, thank you for all your support and love.

My Loving Children Who Would Not Give Up

To my son, Greg, and my daughter, Ramona, who risked their lives day and night desperately searching for me. They never gave up. They have encouraged me to tell our story of how God protected us and how our love conquered all. With love, I am proud and forever grateful!

Thanks to Special Friends

To my devoted friend, Carolyn Koontz, my guardian angel -4. She consoled me during the Federal Court trial and gave me the courage to testify against Erick William Javedon.

To my confident friend, Carol Silaghi, who recognized how desperately I needed help.

To Janice, my roommate in the women's shelter so thankful to heal together!

To Dee Titus Hammon, who, in her Bethel Baptist Bible Study Class ten years ago, gave me the support and encouragement to talk about my hurt. And to many friends from Bethel Baptist Church who encouraged me with their prayers.

Praise the Lord for giving me strength, courage and patience and for His everlasting spirit to heal the hurt. And for His presence so near that showered me with His love and taught me to have faith in Him.

I am so amazed with the Love of God and what He brought me through. He will do it all for you!

In Memory of My Mother
Azalee Virginia Howard Nunn

In loving memory of my precious mother in heaven who lived her life as a prisoner captured in domestic violence-1 but always had a beautiful smile, a lovable laugh, and a soft touch of love in her heart for all. She was a devoted Christian who prayed for her children every day. This book is for my mother and all those suffering from an abusive relationship.

Faithful Friends

Honorable Memorial to the Late Detective John Munden

It is with honor, respect, and gratitude that I thank Detective John Munden for his diligence in the thorough investigation of the horrific crimes committed against me. His concern for the wrong I suffered gave back the dignity I had lost in the evil things I had endured. Thank you, my friend!

Dedication

To the Relentless Efforts of the Late Prosecutor Larry Gossett

With great respect and gratitude, I commend the late Prosecutor Larry
Gossett for his integrity in seeking a conviction for the man who
had committed brutal domestic violence-1 against me. Thank you,
my friend!

Some names in "the predator" have been changed for sensitivity.

To view ARTICLES Go To The Greenfield Daily Reporter newspapeR
www. newspapers archive.org

Why I Wrote About The Hurt That Turned To Hope

Pat E. Robinson

This book is written to show victims that God loves them.
I will never forget what God has done in my life.
My eyes saw His miracles, my ears heard His words, and I wrote them
on the tablet of my Heart. For the Glory to God, I survived!

Draw nigh to God, and He will draw nigh to you (James 4:8).

This is praise and admiration to God, the Lord Almighty—
the King of Glory.

*I will give Praise to Him! Praise ye the Lord, O give thanks
unto the Lord; for He is good; for His mercy endureth forever*
(Psalm 106:1).

THE PREDATOR

By Pat E. Robinson

Patti desires to tell her authentic experience of domestic vio-lence-1 and how God performed miracles that saved her from The Predator.

From the beginning of the reign of terror she experienced, Patti wrote this journal to cope with fear. It is her record of finding strength through faith and how faith gave her peace to endure the evil.

She found that her peace was not the absence of trouble; instead, it was the presence of Christ amid that trouble.

Patti's life turned into horror when she met a man named Erick. In a short time, she realized he was a predator and that she could not escape the deadly brutality she endured.

Erick had a fatal attraction for Patti, and she struggled to escape. For years she was kidnapped, beaten, sexually abused, and controlled by his remorseless evil nature.

She has chosen to share her history of domestic violence-1 that she could not escape. She is a witness of God's Grace as she experienced His intervention and His protection time and time again. He gave her strength through His love and care for her. In her testimony, Patti wants you to see the prayers she prayed and the ways God answered her pleas.

Patti had always been independent and fearless, strong-willed, emo-tionally resilient, and able to deal with stress, grief, loss, and other difficulties until the predator turned her life into a "Reign of Terror for years."

Patti survived through the power of God's love and learned what her faith in God could do for her. She knows He is willing to help those who believe and have faith in Him.

She found that when you draw close to God with your faith, prayers, and heart, God will draw close to you with His protection, guidance, and love.

TABLE OF CONTENTS

INTRODUCTION TO ABUSE

As far back as her memory can go as a child, Patti had memories of something that frightened her. Something was an uneasiness, and if it flashed into her thoughts, she pushed it into a dark place. As she got older, a realization of the tragic domestic violence-1 in her family began to unfold.

Patti was six years old, her brother, Jim, was five, and her sister, Paula, was four when a beautiful lady and handsome man came to visit them one summer day. The couple took the three of them for a long ride to get ice cream. While driving around, the lady and man told them they were their mom and dad. The beautiful lady and handsome man promised the three children that someday they would be coming back to take them to Ohio to live with them.

The new mom and dad went away that day, but Patti, Jim, and Paula were confused. The "mom" and "dad" they lived with and loved were not their parents! It was a confusing time in the young children's life.

They waited for the new mom and dad to come and take them home with them to Ohio.

Years went by as Patti, Jim and Paula waited, but the realization crept in. Their new mom and dad did not come for them. They waited so long.

They remained with the great aunt and great uncle they knew as mom and dad. They always loved them and their happy life in the Appalachian hills of beautiful Southeastern Kentucky near Cumberland Gap National Forest.

Five years later, Patti, Jim, and Paula's mother and father returned to Kentucky to take them to live in Ohio. Patti was eleven, the oldest brother Jim was ten, and sister Paula was nine.

Their parents were packing to take them away early the following day. While the parents packed their clothing that evening, Patti had a desperate feeling to go and hide. She was not going! At the age of eleven, Patti ran away.

Deep down inside, Patti knew something awful kept her from wanting to go live with them. She remembered visions of her mother having black eyes and bruises. It was violence-1 that she had seen! So, at eleven, Patti decided she was not going. Not Patti!

That night, Patti sneaked out of the house and started walking on a lonely country road. She was in a mountainous area, and it was total darkness. All she could see was the moonlight on the pavement before her feet. She feared being abducted by someone on this dark, rural road, so she jumped into bushes and briars as cars approached.

After five or six hours on the road, she was getting exhausted. She then realized she was near her Aunt Juanita's house on Highway 119. Her aunt moved here temporarily while building a new home. This was a blessing. It was dawn when she decided to stop. Patti walked up to the porch and knocked on her aunt's door.

Her aunt was horrified when she answered the door and saw the scratches and bruises Patti had gotten from jumping into bushes on the side of the road to hide from cars. Aunt Juanita listened to Patti's story, and then she made a call to Patti's aunt and uncle. Patti was scared as she sat there on the couch, knowing she was in trouble and sure they would be mad. After a while, her aunt and uncle came to Aunt Juanita's and took Patti back home with them.

It was done! Patti remained with her aunt and uncle. Her mother and father took her sister, Paula, and brother, Jim, away with them to Ohio. When Patti realized her brother and sister were gone, she cried for days because she missed them. She was very lonely.

Years later, her parents had two more daughters, Regina and Pamela, and she would see them and Jim and Paula on holidays and summers when she would visit. Throughout the years, the siblings have stayed close, are very loving, and care deeply for one another.

Patti stayed safe at her home in Kentucky with her aunt and uncle, who were good moral parents. They were hard-working, well-educated, and outstanding citizens. Patti graduated high school, married, and moved away with her husband.

Patti's life was filled with difficulties: an adulterous marriage, children, and divorce. She was fortunate to continue her education and became a strong independent woman with a promising career in the government and a lovely home in an urban area.

As an adult, she visited with her family in Ohio often. During those visits, her brother and sister began talking about the abuse and the times they'd had to rescue their mother when their dad was beating her. Patti knew her father was a binge drinker and an aggressive abuser. Domestic violence typically co-occurs with alcohol abuse.[1] Patti realized her mother was being assaulted and in danger.

The World Health Organization (WHO) statistics indicated 1 in 3 women experience violence in their lifetime. And it is the major cause of injury to women.[2] This pattern of abuse haunted Patti.

One summer day, Patti visited with her mother and felt the need to ask her why she didn't get a divorce and get out of the abuse. Patti was shocked at her mother's answer. She said, "Because sometimes he is good. He tells me he loves me! I love him!" Patti could not believe her mother's words and thought she had to do something to help her mom. Patti knew her mother was submissive. In addition to being abused for years she had a belonging need because she'd lived in an orphanage in her young life with her sister Juanita.

Ultimately, Patti knew at the age of 21, she had to rescue her mother from her domestic predator. So, she made the arrangements and relocated her mother and two younger sisters to Indiana into a house one street away from her house. Her mother was never beaten again.

In the last year of her father's life, when he became terminally ill, Patti had the privilege to care for him. She found it was a healing process for both her and her father. He was a compassionate, thoughtful, kind, caring father and grandfather. Patti knew he was a Christian, and he had been saved. She wanted him to be comforted, so she called a brother-in-law, Pastor Don Messer, to pray with her father in his last hours. Patti and Jim, her brother, were by their father's side when he passed away.

As adults, Patti, her sisters, and her brother have realized the tragic realities of relationship abuse they'd lived as children. It has been painful and draining to watch the people in their lives abuse or be abused. The five siblings missed out on growing up together in a loving relationship. In that regard, all of their lives were impacted. There are times they talk about their stolen family life together. As adults, they are all still healing but blessed to be together with lots of love.

Years later, despite knowing the signs of domestic abuse, it happened. Patti's domestic predator entered her life. How could this happen?

Patti was not prepared for the deadly abusive brutality that she endured. She thought, *NO! Why me, Lord? Why?*

It took years for Patti to know the "*Why*"; the why was when God brought her through something that increased the foundation of her *faith* in Him.

You will see Patti's life lessons unveiled with a clear perception of the miracle of God's blessings. God was there to protect her when she was in danger, and Patti learned to have faith in Him. It is important to remember that domestic violence-1 comes in many forms. Domestic violence is an abusive, violent, coercive, forceful, or threatening act or word inflicted by one family member, household member, or other.[3]

1

A January Blizzard

O n a winter day in January when the snow was falling in blizzard
conditions leaving high drifts on Patti's driveway, her teenage
daughter, Ramona, phoned a business to scrape off their driveway. A snow
removal man came and removed the massive snow drifts and ice from
Patti's driveway. Patti met him in the garage, thanked him, and wrote a
check to Erick Javedon for payment.

Every time it snowed, Patti's driveway was cleared of snow and ice
that year. She did not request the snow removal service, but each time it
snowed, the driveway would be cleared early, before she awoke.

Several years later, after the first clearing of her driveway, Patti received
a call from a man who introduced himself as Erick William Javedon and
said, "Just call me Erick." Erick told her he had gotten a divorce and was
single. He was successful when he owned a truck and auto repair shop, a
wrecker service, and a machine shop business.

He asked Patti if she remembered that he had kept her driveway
cleared one winter some time ago. Of course, she recalled. Patti told
him she appreciated that he removed the snow from her seventy-five-foot
driveway. She thanked him for removing the snow and for his efforts.

He then told her that he had read in the *Greenfield Daily Reporter*
about her divorce and asked her to meet him for coffee sometime. From
the beginning, he was such a charmer, and Patti was immediately very
attracted to him.

Unbeknownst to Patti, the fatal attraction had begun.

1

Erick was extremely friendly and very polite when they first met. They went out to eat and to the movies. Looking back, he seemed fascinated with her and wanted to spend every minute with her. But his kind, polite, attentive demeanor masked what was happening. Since they were both busy, they spent little time together but they did go out occasionally.

In a little time, Erick became somewhat possessive as he always called to check where Patti might be if she was not home, and he wanted her to call him if she stopped somewhere. Patti thought it was because she worked two jobs and had little time to spend with him.

In a conversation later, Erick told her he had dreamed of her since the first time he met her in the winter years ago. He told Patti that he had driven by her house at times and knew she was married, and he had seen her husband and her two daughters and son in the yard. He told her he had seen the big speedboat in the driveway on occasion. She was surprised he had driven by her house to view her and her family. She did not yet understand his obsession.

2

THE CAR ACCIDENT–PAIN JOURNEY

Patti started seeing Erick in January and only a month later, in February she was involved in a head-on car wreck and suffered severe injuries to three cervical vertebrae.

Erick Javedon showed up at the hospital and told her he had gotten the wrecker service request to tow her car to an auto body shop. He owned Erick's Wrecker Service and received the call from the sheriff's department to tow her car to a wrecker shop. Since her car had been towed he offered to take her home from the hospital that evening.

Patti did not realize that the accident was the beginning of a two-year recovery period as she healed from her injuries.

Patti suffered in so much pain that she frequently would need to have pain injections at the hospital for relief. After a painful time, she was scheduled for a cervical discectomy to fuse three vertebrae. Patti was in a full neck brace to support her fusion of the three vertebrae for months. Recovery was a slow process and required extensive physical therapy. Patti had heating pads and massage therapy for several months for her neck injury. In addition, she had painful episodes that sent her to the hospital for treatment.

Patti was so pleased to have Erick come and spend time with her. He was so helpful and concerned. She was ten years older than Erick, yet he was interested in being with her. She was thrilled by his attention.

Erick was attentive and regularly came by her house to check on Patti. He was so kind to help. However, Patti's injuries left her isolated from daily connections with family, friends, and co-workers. She spent over two years in a recovery process from her car accident, during which she was unable to work, suffering physically, mentally, socially, and financially. Erick was one of the few people who offered her human connection and help.

However, you will see throughout this challenging time that she depended upon God for her survival and witnessed His miracles.

3
1992–The Domestic Violence Pattern Begins

While Patti was in a full neck brace to support the three fused cervical vertebrae, she was extremely fragile physically. Over one hundred sessions of rehabilitation followed surgery. During this two-year time, she was unable to work. This caused her to become extremely fragile financially and socially. It was the perfect storm for a predator to swoop in and take advantage of her fragility. Behind the façade of caring, attentive behavior, Erick worked his way deeper into Patti's life, where he would soon show his true colors.

Since Erick was his business owner, he could drop by Patti's house anytime, day or night. One day, just after he'd visited, Patti noticed a wire sticking out from under her couch. She looked and was shocked! She found wires connected to a house phone next to her couch. She was distraught as she looked throughout her house and found that he had wired all the phones in her house to record conversations on phone calls and with anyone coming inside her home.

Patti confronted Erick as to why he had put wires on her phone. He said, "Patti, you are all alone the times when I can't be here with you. I care for you, and I'm only trying to protect you." With his *charm,* he convinced Patti he was concerned for her and telling the truth. Erick said, "Patti, I want to protect you and keep you safe." He was standing there looking so loving at her. Patti saw it as love. She accepted Erick's surveillance as a caring gesture. Erick said, "Honey, you should appreciate me more for taking care of you!" So, Patti thought she had overreacted; after all, he did take care of her.

Erick was beginning to take control of Patti, a victim who had been injured severely in a car accident and suffering physically, mentally, and socially; a victim having some financial hardships due to her inability to work. Although she was covered with a pro-rated Long Term Insurance Policy provided by the Indiana Department of Environmental Management (IDEM), where she was a Senior Systems Analyst in the Information Technology Department, it did not match her pay and slowly decreased over time. She didn't have Erick pay bills or purchase food.

Ultimately, Patti was physically unable to stand up to Erick, and emotionally, she was unable to withstand his threats. He used this most vulnerable time in her life to establish himself as the one in control of her life. She became isolated both by her injury and this man. Erick quickly became abusive, violent, coercive, forceful, and threatening, which constituted domestic violence. She realized she was a victim of domestic violence and found herself with seemingly no way out.

Erick did not want Patti to talk with family, friends, or co-workers. He drove by Patti's house throughout the day to see if anybody was with her and even checked her mailbox. He became extremely obsessive and abusive and threatened Patti regarding her family. He threatened to hurt them if she told anyone or tried to report his abuse. He threatened to harm her daughter, son, grandchildren, and mother if she tried to get help. He warned her that he would put poison in their food or it would be a hit-and-run accident. This predator said he knew where her grandchildren attended school—and it would be easy for him to hurt or even kill them. Patti did not know what to do or where to turn in her helpless state.

Patti's fragile health condition created a perfect situation for this evil man to keep her prisoner and abuse her. She could not involve her family. He would harm them. Her only sanity at the time was to keep a chronicle of the violent attacks as they happened, feeling that having her record would help her family understand her situation if something happened to her. She feared for her life and the lives of her family members.

To keep her bound and controlled, Erick continually described how he would put poison in her family's food if she dared to tell anyone. He planned to inject it with a chemical when they were grocery shopping. Patti had a granddaughter just a few months old and two young grandsons. Erick mentioned he knew where their elementary schools were and that he could pick them up from school.

Erick became even more controlling, jealous, and abusive as time went on. Ultimately, Patti found herself in this unbelievable situation, a prisoner in her own home. There was no doubt in her mind that Erick owned her.

As far as Patti could see, getting out of her abusive situation was not going to happen. It had become a Pattern.[4] Erick was verbally abusive. He blamed her for his violence, and peace would be restored only if she submitted to his demands. So, Patti constantly repeated, "You are right; I am wrong."

Patti was mentally, physically, and sexually abused during those two years by this predator. Her only sanity at the time was to pray. She could not confide in anyone, but she could record incidents, which provided a mental outlet for her, and she could pray.

As she prayed, Patti put her situation in God's hands. God gave her the strength to make plans to survive. She had confidence that God loved her and that He was guiding her back to good health, her job, and her life and family. She knew God would help her escape from this evil man. All the time she prayed, she concentrated on working hard to improve her health and felt God had put her plan into place. In her confidence, He had given her peace.

4

THE BRUTAL BEATING—JULY 1992

The Annual Hancock County 4-H Fair had been in town for a week, and Sunday was the last day before the fair would be pulling up stakes and rolling out of town. Patti mentioned to Erick that she wanted to go to the fair Sunday. He told her he would be too busy to take her. She said, "It is the last day." He told her, "You do not need to go!"

Up to now, Erick had been comfortable with Patti's exclusive dependence on him. She knew he had complete control over her and wanted to keep her isolated, but she tried to break out of his power over her. In the months since her accident, his Pattern of coercive behavior reflected an intentional effort to impair her psychological integrity seriously.[5] She had not gone anywhere in months, but he refused to take her when she mentioned she wanted to go to the Hancock County 4-H Fair. Patti showed courage and told him she had asked Judy to go with her. Again, he warned her not to go.

Sunday, July 13, 1992, arrived. It was a beautiful day, so Patti decided to move forward with her plan and go to the Hancock County Fair. She called Judy. Patti drove to Judy's house, picked her up, and went off to the fair.

They were at the fair for only a few minutes and were deciding what to do first when Patti spotted Erick and a woman together. Immediately, she realized he was with Jessie, his wife! Erick had told her a few months earlier that he had gotten a divorce because he loved Patti. Patti realized Erick did not want her to see him with his wife; that was the reason he did not want Patti to be at the fair. This was a shock to her. Erick turned and saw Patti. He looked enraged. She knew that look. She remembered his warning not to go to the fair. At that moment, his deceit about his marriage hit her hard. Patti never wanted to be involved with a married man ever.

Patti wanted a way out now that she knew Erick was married and that he had lied to her and had not gotten a divorce. Patti thought she could use this reason to tell him why she would not see him again. She decided at that moment that she had no intention of being in this situation one minute longer and had to end it.

Patti knew Erick had told her not to go to the fair, and he would be furious that she was there. Patti quickly grabbed Judy and told her they needed to leave and hide somewhere for the rest of the day because this man would be looking for her and he would be abusive. They immediately left the fair. Patti knew Erick would be fueled with anger. She could not go to her house. Not knowing what to do, she drove around for hours visiting with friends until exceptionally late into the night. Hungry and tired, Patti and Judy finally decided to get something to eat around 1:00 a.m. They stopped at the Waffle House on State Road 9, a local restaurant in Greenfield.

Inside, they saw an old friend, Charlotte, who had moved away from Greenfield a few years ago and remarried. Patti and Judy sat down with Charlotte and chatted with her.

Charlotte talked about some strange things with her new husband and his son. Her husband had become jealous of his son and accused them of having an affair.

Since Charlotte shared her relationship issues, Patti told Charlotte she was hiding from Erick. She explained how he had told her not to go to the 4-H Fair, but she had, and Patti told Charlotte she had seen him with his wife. As she talked, Patti realized she was afraid for her life. Erick had warned her, and he would now be furious that she'd gone to the fair. Patti knew he would beat her if he found her.

She told Charlotte and Judy she would set the alarm system as soon as she got inside her house, and if he broke in, the alarm would go off and alert the Hancock County Sheriff's Department. Hopefully, they would arrest him and take him away.

Judy had been with Patti hiding from Erick for over twelve hours, and they both were looking forward to going home. Patti thought it was so late; it was 2:00 a.m., and Erick was probably home, so she felt it would be safe for her to go home.

Across the room, a group of local police officers was eating and chatting lively. Patti felt much better knowing the city police were inside the restaurant. She thought about confiding in them about her fear of Erick, but she did not because they were Greenfield City Police, and she lived in the county where the county sheriff's department had authority.

Patti, Judy, and Charlotte had gotten their food and were eating when a waitress came to the table and said there was a phone call for Patti. Patti hesitated. Could it be Erick? How would he know where she was? She went to the wall phone in the front of the restaurant and said, "Hello." It was Erick, and he was furious that she had gone to the fair and had seen him with his wife. Patti explicitly told him she would not see him again. She told him she would go to Jessie and tell her he had lied to her about getting divorced. She said she would be honest and tell his wife that their relationship was not good and she had wanted out long ago. Patti felt Erick would have second thoughts about continuing their relationship if he knew Jessie would know about Patti. Patti thought what a great way to get him out of her life. If Jessie knew what Erick had been up to, she would stop him from coming, and Patti would be free at last. Still, Patti was feeling uneasy. Erick needed to be in charge and did not let anybody tell him what to do.

After eating, Patti decided to go home. She dropped Judy at her house and said, "I'll call you when I get home. If you don't hear from me, then call the sheriff's department and have them check on me."

Patti wondered how she had gotten to this place in her life. There had been an attraction, something about him like his smile, muscular

11

build, great strength, attention, something? Why did she have this deep down inside love for him? Why did she feel this almost fatal attraction for him? He had a pattern the same thing every time—control, abuse, apologize, control, abuse, apologize! This was the pattern, and no matter how truthful Erick seemed, his behavior never changed.

As Patti drove out of Greenfield and headed north onto the county roads to her house, she held her breath and scanned the street for Erick's car. She was exhausted and anxious to get home and so glad to press the garage door. *Safety!* She pulled inside her garage. Immediately, a car zoomed up quickly right into the back of her car. She had gotten out of her car. It was Erick. Patti was feeling faint. She was hoping Judy would call, and if she did not answer, Judy would call the sheriff just like they had planned. Patti ran for the door, but it was too late to get inside.

She told Erick, "I'm not going to see you again!"

He said, "You will, or you'll die."

Patti was thinking, *"Hurry, Judy! Call!"* But Judy must have forgotten because she did not call. Erick was yelling that she would not break off the relationship. "When I tell you don't go somewhere, then don't go!" His appearance was strangely evil-looking. His eyes were squinted, and he was yelling and cussing with his fists in her face.

Patti knew she was in trouble. She had not made it inside her house to set her alarm. Erick grabbed her by the hair and pulled her back toward the car. She wrestled with him in the garage. He twisted her arms behind her back, pulled her hair, and kicked her into the car. It was his customer's car. He always had access to customers' vehicles from Erick's Auto and Truck Repair Shop that he owned. Patti realized he could never be traced by anyone looking for her because he had used a customer's car. No one would know the car he had taken her in.

Erick drove out of Patti's driveway and down dark county roads, brutally beating her while driving recklessly. His face looked distorted. He was cursing and furious. She told Erick, "I'm not going to see you again!" He said again, "You will, die!"

Then he stopped on the side of a very secluded dark road and began hitting her in the face and grabbing her neck. She thought he would break her neck at the vertebrae fusion, and she pleaded for him to stop. He said, "You will always be mine, or you die!" This fueled his need to hit her harder. With one blow, he struck her with his fist and knocked her into the car window. Patti felt the pain as the blood gushed out of her nose. She panicked. She could not breathe. She could not see out of her eyes. Patti prayed to God for help! It was so dark and secluded that she thought she would be killed and left on a deserted roadside. Erick indeed was a predator, like a wolf ready to tear her flesh apart with his claws and snarling teeth.

After some time, the raging ordeal ended, and he drove Patti back to her house. Patti was in shock. She did not want to know how bad her injuries were. Her clothes were torn and bloody; she was dizzy and could not fight back. She thought she would be killed now in her own house at the hands of Erick. Suddenly, Erick pushed her into the shower and ripped the torn, bloody clothes off her. After the shower, he took the bloody clothes, put them in a bag, and burned them. He was getting rid of the evidence: no bloody clothes, no car with her blood inside it. Unbelievably, the next shock was just as horrible. He made her dress and again forced her back into the car. She could not believe he was taking her out again through the dark county roads.

Patti was so horrified. He said, "You are mine; you will be mine or die!" This time he had done too much to her. She knew he was planning to kill her and push her out of the car. He was taking her somewhere to kill her where there would be no evidence. Patti was sure that was what he had been planning since the shower. There was no evidence; he washed it down the drain and burned her clothes. Erick had used a customer's car to abduct Patti and brutally beat her. No evidence. There was no way to track Erick when he had Patti in a customer's car.

It was getting harder for her to breathe through her swollen nose, and she could not see because her eyes were so swollen. Patti tried to breathe slowly and control her anxiety. She just kept praying to God. She thought she had lost consciousness at times. The reality was too much for her to grasp when she knew the inevitable consequence.

Patti felt so lifeless. She did not realize that, at some point, he drove back to her house.

He had beaten her so hard her body was bruised all over. She felt an incredible pain that crushed her nose and eyes. At the same time, a part of her consciousness was wholly detached, without feeling, as if she was observing this situation outside herself. Maybe it was survival mode, or perhaps she was in shock, but it was as if this nightmare were happening to someone else.

When he took her inside her home this time, he did not leave. Just knowing he was there made her stomach sick. She wished he would go away, but he stood over her bed and looked at her. She could not understand what he was planning. He just walked the floor around her, lying on her bed and staring at her for hours. She could see this helpless body lying there, with a vulture hovering over it, ready to attack the prey. At that time, she had an out-of-body experience as if she were not there. She was somewhere else watching this all happening.

She felt as if Erick was Satan himself! He was so profoundly immoral that he must be connected with the Devil or another powerful destructive force. He was not behaving like a human. He had no remorse and no compassion. He only had rage and was bent on destruction. Patti was in shock. She could not think. She was emotionally distressed and had a disconnection from consciousness.

As this raging predator continually paced around the room throughout the night, he warned her not to get medical help or go to the police. By dawn, he warned, "GO NOWHERE AND TELL NO ONE! Do *not* go to the hospital or the sheriff." He said he would be watching and hurt her family if any of them came to help her. Patti believed him. Having experienced his rage, she knew he was capable of hurting her family.

Erick stayed until the break of the day. When he left, Patti was exhausted mentally, physically, and emotionally. She waited for a sound before she even thought of moving. She felt so relieved that he was finally gone. Even though he was gone, Patti was frightened. She knew he could come back anytime, and she could not fight him.

She could not even imagine how or why this brutal beating had taken place. It was so surreal. She thought *He beat me because I said, NO, I will NOT see you!* Her thoughts were racing. She thought, *This is not over! He will be back! I need to get help! But how?*

Though Patti had been experiencing what Erick was capable of throughout their relationship, she was in no way prepared for the deadly abusive brutality she had just endured. She thought, *NO! Why me, Lord? Why?*

Her deep down feelings were raw to the bone inside: hurt, shame, hopeless, agitated, depressed, anxious, belittled, unhappy, scorned, helpless, frightened, and grief-stricken. She suffered physically, mentally, socially, and metaphysically, but she knew in her heart Jesus cared for her. Her grief and suffering touched his heart.

Patti thought of this Scripture, *"In God, I have put my trust; I will not be afraid" (Psalm. 56:11).*

Her deep-down feelings were set free with God's loving care. Patti slowly tried to raise herself, but it took much effort. Erick brutally beat her simply because she said, "She would not see him again."

Feeling faint, Patti slowly was able to get up. She got up, passed by the mirror, and gasped when she saw herself. She knew she had to get herself to the hospital. When she got to the top of her stairs, she sat down and slid down each one, step by step, until she was in her foyer.

Patti opened the door to the garage, and she cried in disbelief. The hood of her car was open, and she could see that Erick had torn the engine wiring apart so that she could not leave. She collapsed on the foyer steps. Her only thoughts were, *"No help; no car."*

What happened next was the strangest thing. The front door opened, and Patti's heart stopped as she thought, *Oh, God. He's back!* Patti prayed, *God, please protect me!* She was paralyzed with fear. She thought Erick was returning. It was a living nightmare, and she wanted to wake up. Was he back to beat her more or to kill her? She could not endure anymore. Then she remembered, *"The Angel of the LORD encamps around those who fear him and delivers them"* (Luke 2:10).

Then, the door opened, and Patti saw it was Jessie, Erick's wife. She came inside the door. Patti did not have anything left in her even to imagine this. She was in shock and sick. Was Jessie there to finish the job? Was her rage going to be just as brutal as Erick's rage? Jessie saw that Patti was severely beaten, and her nose and eyes were swollen and bloody. Jessie gasped.

Jessie told Patti, "Erick said to come to your house and see if you were dying." Then Jessie called Erick on her cell phone and said, "She's alive, bruised, and her nose and eyes are swollen!" Their conversation about Patti's condition continued as Patti tried to decide if Jessie was a friend or a foe.

When she finished reporting to Erick, Jessie told Patti that she had endured beatings from Erick for years and tried to escape but could not. Patti knew they were trapped in this together because they knew how evil he was. There was a deep understanding of what they had experienced at his hands.

The door to the garage was standing open, and Jessie saw the damaged wires hanging out of Patti's car. She knew Erick had pulled them out to keep Patti from leaving for help. Jessie entered the kitchen and brought ice for Patti's nose and eyes.

It was clear Jessie recognized Patti needed help. It was strange to be in this situation. Both women understood what each had been through. Both knew Erick was a violent, outrageous predator and that escaping this abusive situation would not happen. They were like sheep, trapped by a pack of vicious wolves intent on tearing their flesh and bones. They were dead meat.

Jessie was concerned about Patti developing blood clots from her badly bruised face and broken nose. She told her to go to the hospital soon. *"Really?"* thought Patti. *"How?"* Patti felt strangely void of feelings.

Jessie and Patti heard Erick's truck. He was coming back. Before he came inside, Patti got inside the coat closet to hide. Patti heard Erick come inside, and she heard Erick and Jessie talking about her. Jessie was saying, "I think she will live."

Patti heard Jessie's car and Erick's truck leave in a bit of time. Jessie must have convinced Erick that Patti was okay to take care of herself. She sat inside the closet for a long time. She did not want to come out.

She was still in shock and could not think. She did not know what to do. Erick had warned her not to leave her house or try to get help. Patti did not want to die. She knew she had to get to the hospital. She could not involve her family, including her brother, Jim, or her son Greg. Erick would lure them into a trap and harm them if she called them. Her daughter just had a baby girl. Erick had threatened that he would hurt her children and grandchildren. Patti knew he was so evil. He would do it. She recalled that Erick told her he had beaten a woman and left her on a county road near Cumberland, Indiana, many years ago. Erick had used this retelling of his past abuse of women as another way to breathe fear into Patti.

After Jessie and Erick left, Patti prayed to God for help. She could not think of how to get help that day. Exhausted, she finally fell into a deep sleep.

5
God Answered Her Prayers for Help

Patti awoke to the phone ringing and quickly answered because if it were Erick, he would get upset if she didn't answer immediately. Thank God it was Carol, the secretary from the office Patti worked in at the Indiana Department of Environmental Management (IDEM) downtown at the Indiana Government Center. She had called about a project that Patti had been working on from home and needed to bring out a PC to communicate to her office.

It was difficult for Patti to talk due to her swollen nose, and Carol sensed something was wrong. Patti had talked about Erick's violent behavior to her before. Carol knew something was wrong with Patti and did not accept her plea, "No, don't come." Patti knew Carol could handle the situation and would not panic. When she explained how Erick had beaten her badly, and he threatened her not to report anything, there was no stopping Carol.

Patti explained Erick's threats, that Carol could not be seen coming there, and told Carol to park down the street and go into the back door by the patio. Late that evening, Carol parked down the road and walked to the back of Patti's house. It was dark when she came in with a plan, determined to help. Carol is a no-nonsense kind of person. She had dealt with exceedingly tricky situations in her lifetime. Patti always admired her strength and outlook.

Knowing she was the one that could handle things, God had miraculously sent Carol. Patti could not logically explain Carol coming to help but knew the experiences in Carol's life prepared her for this. Her composure was so calm, direct, and caring. Patti just knew God had sent Carol. She was exactly the help she needed.

When Carol got to Patti's house, she took over. Carol knew she needed help. She was bloody, her face was severely swollen, and she was in shock. Without hesitation, Carol took Patti to the Hancock County Sheriff's Department to report the attack. Patti knew Carol was an angel sent by God to help her. He had answered her prayer.

It was a comfort to think this would be over soon, and he would be out of her life. Deputy Bridgett Foy took Patti to the Hancock Hospital, and they photographed her injuries.

Patti realized Erick did not know she had reported his attack to the police. She was getting calls from Erick, still warning her not to report anything to the hospital or the police. He surely would return with a vengeance if he knew she had reported it.

Hancock Hospital referred Patti to St. Francis Hospital to have her nose set. The big concern was how she could find someone to drive her there. Patti could not ask her family, fearing that Erick would harm them. She was at a loss about getting to the St. Francis Hospital in Indianapolis.

That day God answered Patti's prayer when she got a call from Charlotte. As she talked, Patti realized Charlotte had some real troubles. They both needed a friend to talk with.

As it turned out, Charlotte offered to take Patti to the hospital and bring her home. This was a good solution since Erick would not know her or recognize the car. No one was aware she was in town. Patti knew God had provided Charlotte to take her to the hospital. It was strange that Patti never heard from Charlotte again. It is a mystery. No one has heard from her.

Patti knew God sent two angels, to guard her that day, Carol and Charlotte.

He had answered her prayers just as He promised. How amazing her God had been!

Patti read Dr. Billy Graham's writing *ANGELS* of the fascinating experiences of those

who are confident they have been attended by angels with what the Bible says about angels

from on high.[6]

> *I am going to send an Angel in front of you, to guard you on your way and to bring you to the place that I have prepared* (Exodus 23:10).

6

ANGEL AT THE HOSPITAL

Patti was grateful to get to the hospital. The X-ray technician immediately took her for an X-ray, which confirmed her nose was broken. She was scheduled with an eye, ear, nose, and throat specialist to have reconstructive nose surgery.

Even in the hospital, Patti was so afraid every moment. She could not get the violent beating out of her head. It was as if she had a recording going on, and it was on replay. Patti was afraid Erick might have had someone watching the house, and they had followed her to the hospital.

The eye, ear, nose, and throat specialist, Dr. Brian Johnson, came into the hospital room and asked Patti what had happened. When she told him, tears streamed down his face. He was incredibly sad for her and said a prayer for her. She felt calm and peaceful.

After surgery, Dr. Johnson told Patti she was close to death because the broken bone was so close to her brain. He said she would need to stay the night in the hospital. Patti was so afraid that night in her room that she could not close her eyes. The memories of the vicious beating the night before played over and over in her head in a series of terrible flashbacks throughout the night. Patti just laid there crying and praying. She stared at the clock and could tell by the sound, without looking, if the hand was going up or coming down the clock. She was terrified and could not forget the brutality she had gone through.

*The Angel of the Lord encampeth round about them that fear him, and delieveth them (Psalm 34-7)-*KJV.

A nurse came into her hospital room and said her name was Kathy. She said, "Do not be afraid! I will be here throughout the night and watch you." Nurse Kathy was pretty, petite, and young with long brown hair. In a short time, Patti fell into a peaceful sleep, but she would awake at times, and when she did, Nurse Kathy would walk over to her bedside and hold her hand.

Patti did not wake again until early morning. She wanted to thank the nurse for being with her and comforting her through the night but did not see Nurse Kathy. When the nurse on duty came in, Patti asked if Nurse Kathy had left for the day because she wanted to thank her for being with her through the night. Patti was thankful she had a peaceful, restful, safe night because Nurse Kathy had come into her room in the night to comfort her.

The day nurse seemed puzzled and said they did not have a nurse named Kathy. Patti was sure they did, so she asked at the front desk and got the same answer. "Sorry, we do not have a Nurse Kathy." At that moment, Patti knew in her heart that "Nurse Kathy" was an angel-4 at her bedside, and Kathy had been sent by God that night! *"I will not leave you comfortless: I will come to you"* (John 14:18)-KJV.

She knew the nurse she saw that night who said her name was Kathy was an angel -4 God had sent. She was real. Patti remembered she had talked with her that night. Kathy had held her hand. In the stillness of the night, Kathy brought Patti heavenly peace and comfort. Her heart could hardly contain the thought. *The nurse was an angel! My God heard my prayers, and He sent an angel-4 to comfort me, praise the Lord! Patti thought to herself of the love God had for her!*

For He shall give His angels charge over thee, to keep thee in all ways (Psalm 91:11).

The next day Patti's brother, Jim, came to the hospital and took Patti home with him. She felt so protected being there at his house. Jim cared for her for a few days. They always were remarkably close, and Jim wanted to protect Patti from this evil man. Jim was a robust six-foot-four-inch man who would go after Erick, but Patti asked him not to go around Erick's house and garage.

Patti knew Erick was cunning and would plot a foul plan to lure her brother into Erick's business lot, where he would ambush him and kill him. Then he'd claim he had only acted in self-defense on his property. Erick thrived on the lure and hunt game. He had the advantage. She would not involve her brother.

When Jim took her home, he stayed with her for a few weeks. He drove her to the doctor to remove the nose packing procedure. Patti felt so loved and so comforted spending time with her brother. She became worried about what she would do after he was gone. Patti was at a loss as to what to do next.

Jim suggested that Patti get a protection order. He took her to Judge Clovart to get the protective order to stop Erick. She paid the one hundred dollars in the county court fees for Protective Order Case NO. 30D02-9505 for protection against Erick. Even though she knew it would do little to stop his behavior, she had to try. Judge Clovart issued the "No Contact Order" on both Erick and Patti.

She knew how much her brother loved her and that God had provided this time for her brother to spend with her to shower her with comfort, care, and love to give her time to heal.

I will praise thee with my whole heart (Psalm 138).

7
Breaking Free of a Reign of Terror

According to the World Health Organization (WHO), "Across their lifetime, 1 in 3 women, around 736 million, are subjected to physical or sexual violence by an intimate partner or sexual violence from a non-partner—a number that has remained largely unchanged over the past decade."[7]

The Protection Order she had paid one hundred dollars for was no detour for stopping Erick. Somehow it was considered just a piece of paper. Patti knew the statistics. She could not get help. Erick walked back into Patti's house to terrorize her as if nothing had happened. He dropped in and started with the same typical abuser's story. He said he could not live without Patti and told her how sorry he was for hurting her. He told her he had started going to church and that he and Jessie were getting a divorce. She found this was a lie and becomes a pattern when an abuser lies and turns on the charm.

She could not stop Erick from coming over, and this man's violent, outrageous assaults worsened in no time. It had become his Pattern. He owned her. He was verbally abusive. He blamed her for his violence; peace would be restored only if she submitted to his demands.

In her mind, finding a way out of her abusive situation would not happen.

Her biggest concern was how he always grabbed her injured neck that had been fused with three donor vertebrae. He knew this increased her fear. This man was mentally, physically, and sexually abusing her. Patti had to get help. She needed to get a message to the sheriff's office. She started planning how to get a tape for evidence.

Maybe it was just her imagination because she was nervous about her plan, but she was sure Erick sensed she was planning something. He began making threats of harm to her family if she should try to get help. He continued to talk about how he would put poison in their food by injecting it with a chemical when her daughter and son were grocery shopping.

Patti was enraged and thought, *How could he threaten to do something to them?* She knew she needed to stop him from harming her family and continuing violent attacks on her before he killed her and them.

She became more robust and learned her only hope to escape was to return to her job at the Indiana Department of Environmental Management. Patti planned to escape Erick's clutches each day and kept her plan concealed. She concentrated on her physical therapy to the extreme and knew she was getting healthy and much stronger.

As soon as Patti could remove the neck brace and drive safely, she was ready to implement the plan. She would record his violent attacks and get the tape to the sheriff's department.

One day while driving to her physical therapy, she stopped at the Radio Shack and picked up a recorder, tapes, and a remote starter. She hid the cassette recorder inside a vase on her dresser and put the remote in a bathrobe pocket.

Patti planned to record Erick's violent rages and sexual assault and get the tape to someone who could help. She planned to take her evidence to Prosecutor Dean Marsh's office on her way to her physical therapy sessions. When the opportunity came to get help, Patti was confident that,

with this evidence, the sheriff would have Erick arrested and charged with battery, and she would be free from him. She tested the recorder several times, and it worked; however, she was nervous that he would find it. If he did, he might go off again and kill her.

As Patti knew it would, a time came when Erick's violence started and escalated as naturally as a raging storm. Erick went on a beating, raping rampage, and the evidence was on the tape. She needed to get the tape to the sheriff without getting caught. At her next physical therapy session, she had the opportunity to take her evidence to get help and have Erick arrested.

She talked to the Prosecutor's office and told him she was in a situation where she was beaten and sexually assaulted and had him listen to the tape. He heard, and it was loud and clear. However, when Patti told him Erick Javedon was the man on the tape who was beating and raping her, he said this was not evidence. What more would he need? He could hear the beating screams and Erick's verbal warnings. In addition, Erick had a charge for Battery from the previous attack just weeks earlier when he had broken Patti's nose.

She was devastated. So, just like that, the prosecutor would not help her.

Patti did not understand why he would not charge Erick. Patti had given the prosecutor the tape as evidence of battery and sexual abuse. Even the fact that Erick had a Battery charge against him existing from his previous brutal beating did not seem to matter to the prosecutor.

8
ABOVE CONNIVING

A month later, Judge Clovart summoned Patti to the county court. Erick's attorney presented a Telephone report that showed Patti's home phone number had made calls to Erick's house phone. She was stunned. Patti explained to the Judge that she did not make any calls to Erick's house. She could not explain how the calls were recorded on a telephone report. Judge Covert did not believe her! The judge dissolved the no-contact order. No protection from Erick now!

Patti was in complete shock. She knew she had not made any calls to Erick's home phone. She'd paid the one hundred dollars for her Protective Order. Why would Patti pay one hundred dollars to provide protection against Erick and then call to talk with him?

She had not called him. She was so confused and upset she thought she was having a nervous breakdown. She knew there was no way she'd called Erick. Patti thought she was losing her mind. She tried to tell the Judge she had never called Erick's house at any time after she filed for the protection order. Nevertheless, Judge Clovart was convinced Patti had called Erick because that is what the "evidence" showed.

The situation was absurd. Patti did not want to talk to Erick, and she did not call Erick. Patti wanted to keep the protection order for her safety. It was hard to understand how this had gone so badly for her. She had done everything she could have done to get help. But there was no help. Erick was untouchable.

God knew that Patti needed answers, and a blessing happened on a rainy day when her home phone malfunctioned. There was extreme static on the line, and it would not dial properly. It was essential for Patti to have her phone system working correctly because her alarm system was connected to the phone. She called the phone company, and a technician was sent to fix the problem.

The telephone repair man found a portable base unit that someone had wired to her home telephone main line on the exterior of her home. It was hidden under the deck floorboards. The repair man explained how this handheld phone base unit could be used to make and record calls that would show up on Patti's telephone record. Calls could be made from eighty to one hundred feet away.

His conniving evil mind! Patti knew how Erick manipulated her telephone records, but Judge Clovart had already dissolved the protection order. Without the protection order in force, Erick could come around her house and stalk her without consequences.

Later, Erick boasted how he'd installed the base unit on Patti's deck, then drove by her home and dialed his house phone using the portable handheld phone. That is how he maliciously recorded calls from her home phone to his home phone. Erick would explain how he had constructed recorded messages from an earlier statement on his telephone answering machine and re-recorded it. He explained how he planned to set Patti up so she would be charged with contempt. Erick said he planned to force Patti to tell Judge Clovart that she wanted to get back with him. Also, he wanted Patti to tell the Judge that they were getting counseling and things were working for them.

Of course, Judge Clovart had charged Patti with contempt and canceled her protective order. Erick was an evil, conniving predator.

That had been Erick's plan for getting his charges dismissed. Erick said his attorney agreed it would work, and it *did*! This arrangement meant that Erick didn't even have to be on her property to make calls from her phone, and she knew this meant calls to the sheriff would not protect her. Without a no-contact order, Erick was free to come to her house without being arrested. And when he came again, she was helpless.

9
AFTER THE WEDDING— FURY AT THE LAKE

In the late fall, Erick had insisted on attending her daughter Ramona and Rusty's wedding. So he decided to go to the wedding. While at the reception, Patti was enjoying friends and family when Erick began to get upset if she had conversations with anyone. Patti disregarded his attitude and continued to enjoy friends and family late into the evening. She did not know how he would get revenge later.

A week after Ramona and Rusty's wedding, Erick insisted Patti go with him to Monroe Lake to help winterize his houseboat. He had gotten jealous of male friends that Patti knew at her daughter's wedding and began bringing up the subject while driving to the houseboat. She reminded Erick these were friends of the family she had known for a long time. However, he could not drop the topic. He kept fuming about the incident throughout the day, becoming enraged as the day went on.

Later that evening, Erick decided to take his houseboat for a cruise around the lake before tying it down for the winter. They headed southward toward the dam at Monroe Dam. As the evening wore on, he became enraged at her about her being what he thought was "too friendly." He started throwing ice on her.

It was a chilly day; she became cold. Suddenly Erick's violence intensified, and he flung her off the houseboat at the Monroe Dam at midnight in November.

It was a dark, black night. The lake was ice cold and forty to fifty feet deep at the dam, where the fish were giant. Patti was horrified. The water was so deep, dark, and cold. It took her breath away! When she surfaced, she could not find the houseboat. She was engulfed in fear. Finally, she could see the houseboat, swam closer and located the steps. Erick threw more ice on her as she got close to the boat. Lake water in November can cause hypothermia.

She tried to pull herself up the steps, and he stepped on her hands. It was horrifying! She feared drowning. Why had she thought she could trust him all over again.

She learned that Erick's apology was a part of the Pattern of the cycle of violence in domestic abuse.[8]

The Next Spring: May 1995

When spring of 1995 arrived, Erick wanted Patti to go with him to the lake again. After that fearful night last November, Patti had promised herself she would not go back to the lake. She told him, "No, she would not go to the lake ever! " She did not go to the lake with him for weeks. Erick had been boating alone for most of the spring and had met a couple at the lake, and he seemed to enjoy boating with them.

Patti knew Erick would not tolerate her excuses much longer, and she was right. One weekend in May, Erick forced Patti to go to his houseboat. On the drive to the lake, Patti expressed that she did not like the vulgarity of the couple, Nina and Rob, that Erick had been boating with, and he became very agitated. As he was driving, the violence escalated. He pulled his car over to the side of the road and started hitting her and pulling her hair. She struggled. Then she opened the car door and jumped out.

As he tried to pull her back inside the car, passing drivers began slowing down to see what was happening. Erick pulled away and left Patti there. She knew he would return to get her. He would force her back into his car with the gun he had in his door. He had threatened her with it earlier.

This was in a rural area with no houses around, and she wasn't sure what to do or how to get help.

Luckily, two motorcyclists stopped and asked her if she was okay. Patti told them she had escaped from a man's car and that he had a gun. Patti told them to leave quickly and call the Monroe County Police. She knew if Erick came back and saw her talking to two men on motorcycles, he might harm all of them.

The motorcyclists called the Monroe County Police; however, they would not leave her until the police arrived. As it turned out, they saved her from being captured because later Erick drove by, but he did not stop.

The patrol officer immediately took Patti to the Monroe County Police Department, and Patti made a report. Charges were filed on May 31, 1995, in Monroe County. She was extremely fortunate to have escaped from his car.

While at the police station, Patti called her brother, Jim, and he came to take her home with him. Patti was never going to Erick's boat again, ever! Since charges were filed, Erick did not show up. Erick went alone to Monroe Lake and continued spending his weekends out on the lake with the couple. He boasted continually about their tumultuous times. Patti did not care. She did not want ever to go back. The thought of Erick and the boat being thrown into the deep, dark water again terrified her.

Patti thought she had won and gotten the last word by filing charges in Monroe County, but just weeks later, on June 12, 1995, Erick came to Patti's house and forced her to go to his boat for the weekend again. She was determined not to go boating with him. She knew he would not leave her alone, but she was not going with him. He told her she was going boating and became enraged and began beating and choking her. There was no escaping his violence. She tried to escape, but he grabbed her, pushed her into his car, and drove to Bloomington, where his boat was docked at the Four Winds Marina.

He told Patti that she would party with Nina and Rob, the couple on the next boat slip. Patti told Erick she would not be around them because they were too vulgar and wild and into smoking pot and heavy drinking.

He became furious and pulled her hair. He yelled, "You will be around them because this is the type of people I want to be with!" He continued hitting her and warning her of another time he had thrown her into the lake near the dam at Lake Monroe. He said, "remember it is thirty feet deep at this slip, and you could fall in tonight and drown. Just do what I say, and you will live through the weekend."

Patti knew she was in trouble and needed help. Secretly, she had an extra cell phone her brother had given her to call for help without Erick knowing, but she could not get a signal. She did not have the opportunity to call for help. When they arrived at his boat around 5:00 p.m., Erick again started choking her, pulling her hair, and hitting her back, stomach, and ribs. He twisted her fingers, toes, and arm. Then he put her head in the toilet of the boat. This was just a preview of what he would do to her if she did not follow his plans.

When Nina and Rob arrived, they demanded that Patti drink one of their special drinks. When Patti got the chance, she tossed the drink overboard, making Erick furious.

Later that evening, Nina and Rob wanted to go to the Four Winds Marina's clubhouse and sit in the Jacuzzi. When they got in the jacuzzi, Erick opened a bottle of Jose Cuervo and held Patti by the hair, pouring it down her throat. He kept her mouth closed to make her swallow it. Patti let some of it run out of her mouth by sliding under the water in the Jacuzzi.

She did not know why Erick was doing these things. He knew she did not drink. Patti pretended to be intoxicated. Erick believed she was since she did not drink.

When they returned to the boat, Erick thought Patti had passed out, so he left her in his craft and went to Rob's boat on the next boat slip. Patti wanted to escape, so she quietly opened the window and heard their conversation. Erick said, "I told you, Rob, she doesn't drink, and it would be easy to put her out." Rob replied, "I don't care. I will do anything to her to get a contract with the state." Erick said, "I'll make her. She'll get you a contract. That is what she does. She writes contracts and hires vendors."

What a shock! Patti realized they were all in on this crazy plan together. Horrible! What would they do? They purposely tried to get her drunk. She was trapped. She realized she was in real danger and had to get away.

Since they were in the other boat, Patti knew that now was the moment she could get away to get help. She jumped up and left the boat in a bathing suit running down through the docks past all the other boats. She tried to be quiet, but the boardwalk made noise. Erick heard her, came rushing, and grabbed her, forcing her back to the boat, twisting her arm behind her back, and holding her by her hair. He was violent threatened to push her into the lake again. Patti thought *"People don't even treat animals like this."*.

She hoped other boaters would hear her but then remembered most of the boaters had left. This stormy weekend with thirty-mile-per-hour winds going through the southern part of Indiana. Somehow, she survived the night.

As she was packing, Patti put the strands of her hair that Erick had pulled out inside her clothes bag for evidence.

As they prepared to leave, she confronted Nina and Rob and showed them the bruises Erick had inflicted on her. They did not care. They were aggressors and had been involved in assaulting her. She knew the danger she was in was real and that she would never be back even if Erick killed her, trying to force her to come to this boat. She shuddered when realizing Erick's friends were involved in the abuse.

Then she remembered a fact her friend had told Patti "Every nine seconds in the U.S., a woman is assaulted or beaten."[9] It's a terrifying statistic.

Erick grabbed her bags of clothing and cosmetics when they were leaving the boat. He would not let her have them. She did not want to have problems. All she wanted was to get away from him. He threatened her the entire trip back home, warning her not to tell anybody anything about the weekend.

She tried to stay calm by breathing slowly, taking long breaths, and praying to God that she would make it home. Patti knew this was the last time for her. She would not go there ever again. Erick had tortured her, and now he had accomplices. They were like wolves, and she was their lamb. It was so degrading to have other people involved in planning to harm you. She thought, *"these people are savage."* They used violence to get what they wanted. Her body got goosebumps, and she shivered from knowing the danger she had gone through. God had helped her. She had terrible flashbacks every moment.

Patti had a wellspring of inner strength and could hardly wait until they got to her house, where Erick would drop her off and leave. He always dropped her at her house and then left for his house.

Erick seemed to sense her thoughts. *Did he know she was desperate?* Patti silently prayed and tried to remain calm so he would decide to leave her house that night. She was so devastated by the violence.

When in her garage, Erick checked Patti's purse and found the strands of hair she kept that he had pulled out at the boat. He now knew Patti had planned to use it as evidence. He was furious and destroyed them. Then he decided to stay. He knew she was planning something.

Patti finally realized she was in danger of her life. He was a predator. She thought, *"This was not love."* His charm had blinded her, and he could convince her he was telling the truth and that he was going to change. All lies! *The Abuse Pattern.*[10] She prayed to God to help her escape his clutches completely.

It would seem all hope was lost, but when your only hope is in God, you can rejoice because of who He is: firm, loving, powerful, faithful, all-knowing, and in control. Patti knew that God was in control. *And call upon me in the day of trouble; I will deliver thee, and thou shalt glorify me* (Psalm 50:15)-KJV

10

ESCAPING

Erick was pure evil. He was going to kill her. Now was the time to get away from him.

Throughout the night, Patti planned to escape for help that Monday morning as soon as Erick left her home. She knew he had to get to the business he owned that morning. Patti knew he suspected she would try to get help the minute he left her sight, and he had threatened her that if she left, there would be trouble.

To guarantee she would not leave, he called her home phone to check in every five minutes to ensure she would remain home. He would look for her if she did not answer her home phone. She had to get ready to leave the instant he made the next call. She would had five minutes to leave before he knew she was gone.

She knew he would return the moment he sensed her desperation. She had cried all night silently and could not sleep. She knew she had to escape now.

Patti grabbed some clothes and was ready to leave when she heard his car. Just a moment before he drove into the garage, she stashed her clothes and toiletries in a trash can. Good thing! If Erick had found them, she knew she would have been beaten and chained, and she would be unable to leave.

She ran to the kitchen and busied herself with dishes as Erick walked through and checked the house for signs of packed bags. He threatened her again and then left. He was gone. Her heart was beating so fast, and she knew the time to go for safety was now. With no time to pack extra clothing, Patti jumped into her car. She knew he might be waiting for her just a block away.

She started the car and gunned it out of the garage. She would ram his car if she had to. One moment was all she had to get away before he would call her house phone, and there would be no answer. He would hunt her down. He liked to hunt and trap and show his evil spirit.

Breathe, breathe, breathe! she told herself. Her heart was pounding. Her hands were shaking on the wheel. *Breathe!* As she drove out of her driveway, she instantly thought of how he liked to play his hunting games.

Patti knew she should not drive on the main roads; he would look for her there first. So, as her heart pounded, she headed onto the back roads. She was driving faster and faster, trying to make it to the interstate before he caught her. *Go faster,* she thought. *Drive faster!*

She hoped she had made the right decision to drive the back roads when she noticed two sheriff's cars parked by the road. Right away, she recognized Deputy Bridgett Foy. Patti stopped and explained to Deputy Foy that she was running from Erick Javedon and needed help to get somewhere safe. The officers told her they could only follow her to the end of the Hancock County line, but they could escort her to I-70 at the Mount Comfort ramp.

Patti was exhausted but elated she had the escort to the interstate. She continued on I-70 to Indianapolis. Her head was throbbing from Erick pulling her hair. She decided to stop at her youngest sister Pam's house and have her massage for her hair. Pam saw the bruises on her body where Erick had beaten her over the weekend. She told Patti her hair was stressed where he had pulled out strains of hair. Patti knew she was in shock from trauma.

She explained to her sister that she would be hiding in a shelter and could not be in contact with any family for a time. It was a blessing to see her sister and get hugs, but she had to get to a shelter. Her life had become too big a battle to escape the evil predator, but God had fought the battle for her.

Praise be to the Lord, Our Savior, who daily bears our burdens (Psalm 68:19).

Finally, Patti arrived at her office in the Government Center downtown in Indianapolis. Right away, she called Lena, head of the Indiana Department of Family Social Service Association (FSSA).

When Patti recovered from her automobile accident and returned to work in November, she began planning with Lena to go to a shelter to escape from Erick. Patti had no choice. This time she truly felt it was a life-or-death situation. Lena had been afraid he would kill her and was glad to know that Patti was finally getting away to a safe place.

11

GETTING TO THE JULIAN SHELTER FOR WOMEN AND CHILDREN

Lena remembered her conversations with Patti in November 1994 about getting away from her abuser. As they talked through Patti's situation, Lena started planning for Patti to go that day to the old Julian Center Shelter for Women and Children, located in Haughville, Indiana, an old section of Indy.

They both realized Patti had accomplished some safety planning tips for her circumstances, but she had too little time to complete them. Now the time had run out, and she had thrown her packed bag of necessities and clothes in the trash can when Erick returned.

Luckily, Patti had completed other vital steps. Her accounts were secured, and she had all her bank cards. She had medication, her phone, a charger, and a list of significant phone numbers. She had turned off GPS on her phone and had factory reset it. Now she would stay in a women's shelter and change her routine, as recommended. She would need to be constantly aware of her daily routine and begin to alter it over time. Of course, it is recommended to file for a protection order. However, Hancock County had dissolved Patti's protective order.

Regardless of where someone is in the "leaving process," planning is still needed. It is essential to gather information, even if you are not ready to make a move. It is hard to think straight when you are in a crisis. Putting a plan together ahead of time is best.

Patti told Lena about the terrifying weekend at Lake Monroe. Erick was so evil. He was going to kill her. Patti told Lena she had survived because of her faith in God. She had experienced God's infinite goodness. Still, she wondered why God loved and protected her as He did.

She had barely escaped her predator, but Patti had done it. She had left her home in Cranberry Lake Estates. She was ready to go to the Julian Center Shelter. The shelter was in a predominantly low-income neighborhood, the poorest area in the city. The Julian Center was a Catholic girls' school and residence a hundred years ago. It was very outdated and had no air conditioner. There was only one substantial common restroom with open showers like at public pools.

As she arrived at the shelter, Patti began to feel safer than she had for some time. Immediately, a heavenly peace flooded her heart and soul. She would typically have been in culture shock, but the safe feeling gave her peace. She was exhausted from the violence she had been through for years. She felt thankful for the protection and grateful to be there.

Patti got the key to her room. She read the strict rules: "No food or water in your room anytime. You are required to lock your room when inside and when you leave." This was to keep anyone from looking for drugs and to prevent theft of your items. The most rigid rule for Patti was "No snacks in the room."

The first night Patti was exhausted and fell right away into a deep sleep. She was awakened with a vision. She remembers well, *"her vision of an ocean of women reaching up. It was masses of just their faces. She could see their fear and felt their pain. They were reaching for help."*

Patti has often wondered, *"If her vision was of the many women that had come to this sanctuary for help. Did they get help and are they safe?"* She has never forgotten her vision.

She awoke next morning in her tiny room, with a set of twin beds lining the walls and a baby bed the width of the room. The shower and facilities were in a large, shared bathroom. That first morning, Patti was in bathroom, standing at the sink brushing her teeth, she looked down into the eyes of a small African American boy. They were so sad looking.

Patti smiled, and he smiled back. She and the small boy knew they had been terrorized and felt safe together. Simply safe.

Patti felt she would be safe to drive the short distance to her office at the Government Center. However, she found later that Erick's wife and hired men had tracked her to the Julian center and knew her drive to the IN Government Center. They attempted to abduct her on the way to work. The fact was she wasn't safe anywhere!

Patti's chore was cooking breakfast for forty women and children on Sunday mornings. She loved cooking for them, even the ten pounds of bacon. They loved her bacon, eggs, gravy, and biscuits. She brought lots of smiles to their faces. These women and children all had gone through horrific experiences, and Patti's heart ached for them.

She was relieved to be safe and thankful to God for providing this haven. It had been so long since she could feel safe. The peace that came over her felt like a warm blanket. She was so comfortable here. She had discovered love and appreciation for herself, and it felt good. Thank God!

Though she felt physically safe because Erick could not get to her, she knew it was too good to be true and that he would not leave her alone, and she was right.

That first day at the shelter, Patti suddenly realized Erick had all her accounts turned off. She found he had reported all her banking cards as being stolen. Erick reported her cellular phone stolen. Patti wondered how he did this since her name was on the account. When she called, the representative said it had just been reported as stolen by a man who said the name on the account was misspelled and should have been *Patrick* rather than *Patricia*. *Then* he provided Patti's correct social security number. Erick had stolen her social security number, driver's license, credit cards, and bank information.

Unbelievable. Patti now had no access to her bank accounts or her home's alarm system. Patti went to the bank and filled out the necessary forms to get the new cards, but it would take ten days to two weeks. This was devastating: *no home, no clothes, no phone, no money!* Financial control is another tactic of an abuser. It is another way to make the victim dependent on the abuser for basic needs.

That day, Erick was trying to find her, and he called co-workers, family, and friends. Erick had taken Patti's IDEM staff phone book and called, saying he was Patti's brother and wanted to know if she had been at work that day. He continued his harassment, calling coworkers and family late that night, pretending to be Patti's brother.

Erick harassed her special friend Candy, a coworker, and attorney for IDEM. Candy was petite in size but not a person to be reckoned with. Patti found refuge at Candy's house at times when she was hiding from Erick. And as small as she was, Candy was brave.

No home, no clothes, no phone, no money! Patti wondered if being in the shelter was even worth it if Erick could continue his reign of terror in other ways.

The next day God would prove that He had a purpose for her being in the shelter. A battered victim named Janice checked in at the shelter and became Patti's roommate and friend. They constantly talked about the abuse they had suffered and found that their experiences were similar. They both had horrible treatment from an abuser. It was great rooming with Janice, who was a lovely woman. Janice and Patti spent all their time together and became as close as sisters. It was both an enlightening and healing experience as they each shared the torture of daily, frequent domestic violence and abuse. It was a fantastic feeling to finally be free here at the center and safe from the tragedy of abuse.

After work most days, Patti picked Janice up to go out to eat and shop and enjoy their newfound freedom. Janice had recently retired from ten years in the U.S. Army and carried herself with a military bearing. Janice did not have a job or car when they met at the shelter. Patti brought her personal computer into their room and taught Janice some computer skills to help her get a job. Being able to share with Janice was an encouragement. To know that her friend was placed there by the same God that made our sins as white as snow was indeed a blessing.

Janice was not the only person Patti met at the shelter. A day after Patti arrived at the shelter, an elderly lady came for protection from her husband, who had beaten her badly. The lady had been choked, and the finger marks were still on her neck. She could not move her neck and was in extreme pain.

Patti drove her to Wishart Hospital. As Patti was parking, a car stopped in front of her car, and someone got out of the car and started coming toward Patti's car. At that exact moment, another car pulled close to the driver's side of her car. Patti was ready to turn right into the emergency room entrance to help this lady get inside the hospital. Patti helped the lady out of her car and to the emergency door at the hospital.

She was on her way to work and was trying to figure out why these cars boxed her car in and surrounded her car in the middle of the street. It did not make sense.

After Erick was arrested, his wife, Jessie, told Patti that Erick had hired those men to abduct her. Jessie was involved in the abduction plan, and it was she and two men in those cars that day, but they saw that she was with someone else, so they did not complete their plan. God was there even when Patti was unaware. It was a miracle. Patti was reassured that every day God is with us and protects us. Patti realized Erick had control over Jessie, too. She had been abused for fourteen years, and now he owned her mind, body, and soul.

Praise be to the Lord, our Savior, who daily bears our burdens (Psalms 68:19).

12
Trying to Return Home

One day in May, Patti took Janice with her to get more clothing from her home only to discover she was locked out. All the doors were locked inside Patti's house, and the garage door opener would not work. It took hours to get inside her house. Patti did not doubt that this was another evil act performed by Erick.

Once inside, they found her house destroyed. Erick had broken into her house and vandalized it throughout. Destruction was everywhere. The water in the finished basement was a foot high. All the water pipes had been removed. The water tank was removed, and the sump pump pipes were broken.

Patti could not believe the water destruction Eric had caused inside her finished basement. She reported the destruction to the sheriff's department. Patti would not return home until the water was drained out of the basement. Eventually, the drywall, water tank, pipes, and sump pump were replaced.

The worst devastation was when Patti saw the photo frames lying on the floor. Oh, how she cried. Her heart broke because family photos were her most precious belongings on earth, next to her family. Erick had torn them out of their frames. Erick knew well the value Patti placed on her photos. It is common for abusers to destroy their victims' most precious valuable items. He had already taken so much from her, and now he had taken her lifetime collection of family photos. From picture frames throughout the house to desks and walls and even two end tables with full drawers of vintage photos along with twenty-five family albums . . . all gone. All the frames were lying around empty. He had ripped the professional photos out of the frame. All her family home videos are also gone.

Patti spent the day at the Hancock County Courthouse filing the vandalism claim and the break-in report with the sheriff's office. Janice was right there with her. There was no doubt God had placed Janice in Patti's life. She was a blessing from God sent to protect Patti in many ways. She was military through and through, and Janice was always alert to her surroundings. Months later, when Erick kidnapped Patti, he would ask her how she'd gotten a bodyguard. He thought Janice was an assigned bodyguard for Patti's protection. God had blessed Patti with Janice as her roommate and friend. She had unknowingly become another angel for Patti's protection.

After Patti stayed the maximum time in the shelter, she alternated a night at a time with family and friends. She could only stay one night with anyone, so Erick, Jessie, and the hired men could not track her. She was fortunate the IDEM Commissioner, Kathy Prosser, was relocating to D.C. and offered up her elaborate house in uptown Indianapolis. What a haven.

Patti knew she could not return home until her pipes were repaired. In late summer, Patti's brother-in-law, Gary Rennier, came to her house to fix the pipelines, sump pump, water tank, and other water fixtures that Erick had vandalized in May. While Gary and Patti were at the house, Erick called on Patti's unlisted house phone. She wondered how he got the new unlisted number. Erick threatened her while on the phone. He admitted to having the photos and doing the damage to the house. Patti would hang up the phone, but Erick continually called and threatened her, her car, her home, and her family.

Gary called the sheriff's department, and Deputy Joe Hunt came to Patti's house. Deputy Hunt listened in on the threatening calls, and when he realized Javedon knew he was at Patti's house, Hunt did a fake close-out call to HCSD to indicate he was leaving Patti's residence. When Javedon thought Deputy Hunt had left her house, he became more threatening. Deputy Hunt spent a long time listening and heard Erick threaten Patti, her children, grandchildren, and mother. Hunt heard Javedon brag about vandalizing Patti's house. Deputy Hunt prepared a warrant for his arrest. Patti appreciated Deputy Hunt's diligence in getting the warrant and having Javedon served and arrested.

Javedon was served the arrant and bailed out that day. And he came again after Patti.

13

October 1995 Abducted, Chained, Beaten, Raped

This chapter is especially difficult to discuss. Patti was abducted on October 26, 1995. She was handcuffed, beaten and raped for four days before escaping on October 30, 1995.

It was 8:00 p.m. on Thursday, October 26, 1995, after Patti had returned to her home and was shopping in Kroger supermarket. Erick walked up to Patti in the local Kroger parking lot. Patti was frozen with fear, preventing her from screaming for help or running away. She could not do anything other than stand in silence. It had been a while since she'd escaped from him and his violence.

Erick begged her to listen to him because he said his conscience was bothering him. He said he wanted to talk with her about the family photos he had taken from her home. She remembered the pictures well and the feeling of devastation she'd had when she discovered them missing and her home vandalized. Her mind flashed back to the empty frames lying on her floor. Yes, she wanted them back.

Erick told her he knew how much she valued her family photos and was sorry he had taken them. He wanted to give them back to her. Now, Erick was saying he'd changed and was sorry for all his actions to hurt Patti. He said, "I can't live without you! Patti, I have missed you. Will you believe me?"

Patti was trying to think things through. Yes, she wanted her photos, but he'd said he'd changed, and now he was asking her to forgive him. He begged Patti to believe in him. There in the night, Patti saw something good in him. He had felt bad about taking her photos. She felt deeply attracted to him, and Patti believed he had changed. She was excited he wanted to give the pictures back to her. It was hard not to believe that he had changed even though he had abused Patti.

Why did Patti believe him? Because there was a link between them that began with something when they first met: his *charm,* his *smile,* his *trust,* his *care,* the *good times* they'd shared. Now, in the darkened parking lot of Kroger's, he seemed so nice, like he had changed, and he was convincing Patti that he was telling her the truth.

Erick convinced Patti he felt terrible about taking her precious photos, and she believed him. She trusted him.

This man had a convincing personality. He was a charmer and a liar at the same time. Even though Patti hated his abuse, Erick was able to trick her into going with him to his house. It is hard to admit that Erick misled Patti, and this time she went on her own to his house.

She believed he had changed. This was it, the trap set to gain back his victim. No matter how much the abuser seems truthful, their *Pattern* never changes. Abuse victims want to believe their abuser has changed; however, the reality is the *Pattern* works for the abuser time after time and keeps the victim in his clutches.[11] The trap works because it feeds the victim's emotional need to believe him. Erick was a professional at manipulation, as no one else would ever think this man would do the wicked things he did. At this most *crucial* moment, Patti didn't recognize it. Erick had not changed.

All she heard was, "I miss you." The trap was sprung. Patti fell for this, which is what most women are vulnerable to. This fed Patti's emotional need to believe he had changed and thought he cared. After Erick convinced her that he had changed and had tremendous guilt about what he had done to her, he asked her to drop by his house and pick up all four boxes of her family photos and albums. Now, he stood there and lied.

Why did Patti go to his house? Was it just that she wanted her photos back, or did she want more, perhaps a chance to have their relationship back? Patti cannot explain why she did not just walk away.

She cannot explain why she went to his house that night, but she does remember how much value the large boxes of photos held in her heart.

In her mind, it was as if she were taking her life back by getting them. She believed that by going with Erick, she would have them back.

It's known that abusers take things that mean the most to a victim. Giving back the victim's valuables becomes a *trade-trap* to get the abused victim back. She did not realize it was part of his trap.

When Patti got to Erick's house and he opened his door, Patti saw the boxes of photos sitting just inside his doorway. Yes! She wanted them back, and now they were just within reach. Yes, she trusted him.

She was standing there looking through the door glass, and Erick asked her to hold the door open so he could get the boxes. She did, and that is where the terror once again began. He had set the boxes of photos *just inside the door*. He'd convinced her. He planned this, and it worked—the trap—his fantasy played out.

Suddenly, Erick grabbed Patti's wrist, twisted it, pressed it into the door's frame, and pulled her inside the house. She struggled but could not get away. He hit her on her chest and back. She fought him. He choked her. She tried to escape, but she could not get away. She realized she had been trapped.

Erick had spent lots of time planning every detail of his fantasy. He knew she would fall for getting them back, so he had intended to set the boxes of her precious photos just inside the glass door for her to see. He schemed to snare her. He would have her again. This was what he had fantasized about. It was a thrill for him to know he could trap her like an animal. He had set up the trap and then stalked her that afternoon to the Kroger parking lot. He was on a trapper's high, waiting to set the blood of a trapped animal.

He knew she would listen if he told her he wanted to give her back her four boxes of family photos. He would explain how sorry he was that

55

he took them, and she would believe him. He was the predator setting his trap for his prey. This was a typical control fantasy that abusers used to lure the women into their trap. Patti did not have a clue about the danger she was in.

Erick's **fantasy** is a typical pattern in the cycle of violence.[12] Patti believed Erick and went to his house. This was a mistake. She jeopardized her life. His habitual lies trapped her.

This is the trap abused women fall for many times, and statistics prove how *deadly* it is.

She knew she had made a mistake. Erick kept her through that night, forcing her to have sex.

Why did she believe he had changed? She heard him say, "I have changed, and I miss you." This was her emotional need. Patti blamed herself for falling for his lies.

The next morning, Patti had bruises over her body, but those on her neck and the side of her face were very dark and visible, so Erick forced her to call work to say she was taking the day off. By Saturday morning, she felt intense. She needed to get away! Her bruises had gotten darker over her face and neck, and he would not let her leave. He knew that, with the new bruises, she would indeed have more charges against him for the battery.

On Sunday, he tied her and forced her to go to her house. She knew he had a plan. She thought to herself, *What is his scheme this time?* He pulled clothes from her closet and put them in his car. He vacuumed her carpet to remove footprints before they left. Once again, he left no evidence. He was so conniving, but why?

Then he drove to Myer's Store, and before he forced her inside, he untied her and threatened her not to try to get away. Erick said all he wanted to do was establish that they were together in a public place to make it appear that Patti was with him willingly, and then no charges would be brought against him. She knew he had a gun in his jacket; there was no chance of getting help. There were mothers and children inside the store. Innocent people. No! She would not have a chance of getting any help. It was too dangerous for her and for others to try.

While inside the Myer's store, Erick assured Patti that she could go home when they returned to his house. However, as Patti suspected when they got to his house, he would not let her leave as he had promised. This was day three now! She still had the bruises and marks, and he would not let her go until they disappeared. Patti started to panic as she realized no one knew he had her. *No, no, no,* she thought. She wanted out. Back at his house, she got frightened when he started to get angry again. Patti tried to convince him she would not go to the police on Saturday night and Sunday. And he seemed to believe her as Patti tried to remain calm. All night Sunday, Patti lay awake and tried to leave as he slept. Each time he would wake and stop her. Early Monday morning, she got dressed and was going toward the door. He caught her and pulled her back into the house. She told him she had to go to work, but Erick forced her to call her office and take the day off. She was hoping Candy or Carolyn would get suspicious and call the sheriff because she was out of work on Friday and now out again on Monday. He put her back into his bedroom and locked the door.

After a few hours, Patti thought Erick would go to the repair shop behind his house, but he didn't leave. Later in the morning, Gerald, his garage worker, came to Erick's door for the key to open the repair shop. She tried to escape out of the door. Erick grabbed her and pushed her back, but Patti was sure Gerald had seen her trying to get out the door. She was hoping he saw her bruises and would call the police.

Her heart broke when Erick slammed the door, but Patti knew Gerald had seen her. Hopefully, he would do something to help her. This made Erick furious, and that fury led him to his next horrific act. He made her undress and took her clothes away. He forced her into an exercise room. There he handcuffed her to a large piece of exercise equipment. He then put rubber gloves on and removed her personal belongings from her car that he had taken from her house on Saturday. Then Erick put her clothes into the closet in his bedroom. Patti thought it such a strange thing to do. She discovered his scheme later. He used her clothing to deny that he had chained her in a room at his house and had kept her confined against her will. Erick's plan worked HCSD believed him. He was an evil, conniving predator.

Patti heard Erick tell Gerald on the intercom that "he and Patti were staying in today to be together without interruptions," and both men laughed. Patti's heart sank. Gerald wouldn't be helping her after all.

Patti had been blinded by this man, a predator of women. Statistics show the multitudes of women who have lost their lives in one moment, day, or weekend in a violent attack.

Erick set up a monitoring system between the garage and the bedroom. Patti knew this was so he could listen for any noises she might make to get help. He came into the weight room throughout the day to unlock her handcuffed hands from the weight equipment and to take her to his bedroom to sexually abuse her. If he had a call from his shop worker and had to leave the bedroom, he always cuffed her hands behind her back and chained her feet. This went on all day.

At times, Erick would force her into the other room and handcuff her again to the exercise equipment.

This was too awful; she felt sick. Her stomach was upset, and Patti was having to use the bathroom often, so Erick allowed her to put on his blue bathrobe. Now he was always guarding her even as she went to the bathroom. Patti was so desperate that she thought of breaking through a window and jumping out. He was always calculating her moves and could read her mind. She hoped she would get the chance to jump out the window and run to safety. Although she could imagine the cuts from jumping through a window, landing on the cold white snow, and being free seemed wonderful. Patti wanted to be free of this predator. The day continued with him tormenting her, handcuffing her again to the exercise equipment, then going back into his garage.

Around 3:00 p.m., Erick returned, unlocked the cuffs, and forced her to have sex again. Patti could hear cars coming in and out of Erick's auto shop driveway for repairs. She wondered how the world could just go on while she was terrified and tortured like this.

Sometime later that day, Erick's worker called him on his intercom. It must have been crucial because Erick hurriedly dressed. He did not take time to chain her to the exercise equipment in another room. He handcuffed Patti's hands behind her back as he had done all day, but this one time, he did not chain her feet together. He tied her feet with her pantyhose.

He left her on the waterbed. He had not taken the time to chain her legs or put her in the other room as he had done each time before.

As soon as he went out the door, Patti was frozen with fear by what she was thinking. Could she make a run for help? How could Patti get out of bed without him hearing her on the intercom? Would he be mad enough to beat her to death if he caught her?

Patti's mind was screaming one thought: *NOW! IT HAS TO BE NOW!*

With her heart pounding, Patti rolled to get leverage and momentum, trying to get up over the waterbed rails. She tried and could not raise. Her hands were cuffed behind her back, and her feet tied with her pantyhose. She tried over and over to arch without hands and to get edged with her chin on the waterbed rail. She arched and moved her back up and down. She had to get going before he came back. She was so scared. Patti had to get over the waterbed rails. She was struggling franticly. Now almost over with her chin. Finally, she made it up and over the waterbed rails. Then she fell off the bed onto the floor. This made a loud sound. She was hoping Erick did not hear the noise over the intercom.

With her feet tied and hands cuffed behind her back, she had to get up over the three stairs that led out of the bedroom into the living room. Nudging up the steps on her knees with her legs tied, she rooted with her chin over and over until she got to the top step and rolled over the three steps from his bedroom to the living room. Patti was in the living room with her feet tied. Trying to stand she could not walk. All she could do was hop, trying not to fall. It would be too difficult if she tripped and fell to get up. She thought her heart was going to beat right out of her chest.

When Patti was at the front door and grabbed the doorknob, it turned. Her heartbeat was faster! The door opened. She could see Main Street, U.S. 40. She was so frightened that Erick would grab her any second. Her neck was tight with fear, but the door was open! She saw the U.S. 40 highway. There were three steps. Fortunately, as she jumped off the porch the pantyhose became loose as she landed in the front yard. She could run now. She made it to the end of his driveway. She was at the highway screaming for help with her arms cuffed behind her. Patti was only wearing his blue bathrobe.

Thank God! She was still alive. How wonderful the cold snow felt as it touched her feet.

She called out desperately, "Help, help; please help! Stop!" But nobody would stop. She knew she looked like she came out of a horror movie: bloody, bruised, handcuffed, feet tied, hair stringy, makeup smeared on her face, wearing a man's blue bathrobe. Oh, God, help! "Somebody HELP ME!" But she soon realized that no one would stop.

She had to get help. Patti ran into the middle of the road, flagging a semi-truck driver. She started heading for the front of the semi's cab, but he would not stop. He swerved over to the side of the road, barely missing her. She knew she would rather die here in front of the truck than die in the evil predator's house. She was running for her life. Didn't they know that Erick would drag her back and kill her? Patti kept running west down the middle of U.S. 40 toward the city of Greenfield. She felt her bare feet getting numb. Cars would not stop.

Sometime back, Patti had seen his arsenal of guns he made in his machine shop. She realized the law knew about them. Consequently, they would not help her. It was as if he could get away with breaking the law. And now, if he shot her with a silencer gun, no one could prove he did it.

She was thinking about what Erick would do if he caught her. Erick knew he would be in trouble if she got to the sheriff. To stop her, he could shoot her using the silencer. Was he behind her now? She couldn't look back.

In the book of Job, Satan says to the Lord that he was *"From going to and fro in the earth, and from walking up and down in it"* (Job 1:7)-KJV. Patti knew this was true as God's Word says. Indeed, she had met Satan himself. She did not doubt in her mind that Erick was demonic. Why would any human spend so much evil effort to do what Erick had done? Over and over, Erick had been a conniving, lying, deceitful, vicious sexual predator. He caused overwhelming fear and abuse with his maltreatment. He was *evil* and morally corrupt. He treated Patti, another human being, with complete disregard on a habitual basis: abusing her physically, psychologically, and sexually. And, somehow, after it all, he had remained above the law. This made Patti certain he was operating with the Devil at his side.

Even with all her fear, she blamed herself for believing him. Why did she? This was *The Pattern* with Erick. He always dominated her with his physical violence, sexual abuse, intimidation, emotional abuse, and threats of violence, even to her family.

Patti cried out in the middle of U.S. 40, "Please, somebody help me! Help! Help! Help!" As cars passed by, she kept screaming, "HELP!" Didn't they know Erick would soon show up to drag her back into that house and kill her? Nude, except for the bathrobe, Patti kept running. She knew Erick would quickly be on his way, so she could not stop. He could shoot her with his gun, which has a silencer. She would lay dead by the road, and nobody would link him to killing her.

As Patti kept running, she became breathless, but she remembered the silencers and machine guns, so she pressed on. Patti was near the Central Indiana Power building as an employee pulled into the drive with a work van. He stopped and, without hesitation, helped Patti to the door of the large electrical company and called the sheriff's department. Patti knew she was horrified to look at her. She was beaten black and blue, hair stringing down her face, makeup smeared, eyes puffy from crying.

When the Hancock County Sheriff's Department arrived at the Central Indiana Power Office, they could not open the handcuffs locked on Patti's wrist. She waited while someone came with cutters to cut the handcuffs off her wrists. It felt so wonderful being alive and having her hands free. A female officer, Officer Bridgett Foy, arrived and took her to the hospital for a sexual assault test kit, a photo, and medical treatment. Officer Foy was comforting and compassionate at a terrifying time in Patti's life. Patti was so very grateful for her concern.

Afterward, Officer Foy transported Patti to Hancock County Sheriff's Department, where Detective Kevin Schultz interviewed her and took her statement. Schultz was not friendly at all. He was rude. He did not listen to Patti's statement about the days Erick had held her and did not treat her as a victim of multiple crimes. She was uncomfortable and did not understand his mood, but Patti was too exhausted from days of inhuman torture of the worst kind to try and figure out why Detective Schultz was acting so cynical. This was a natural response because Patti realized Erick had set her up, and it worked. She was beginning to realize the *Pattern* works for the abuser every time.

After what seemed to be a long time, Detective Schultz decided that Patti had to go into Erick's house to get her belongings from him. What belongings! Patti couldn't believe Detective Schultz had her return to where it had been so horrible, but Officer Foy took Patti to Erick's residence. Detective Schultz and three other officers came as well. Patti was more comfortable with Officer Foy and talked about what had happened. Officer Foy told her that "this evil man was in her head," controlling her even when she wasn't with him. Patti knew how terrified she was when she was captured, beaten, handcuffed and sexually assaulted.

When Detective Schultz arrived at Erick's residence, he would not allow any of the three officers to accompany him inside. Officer Foy did not understand why Schultz requested the other officers to stay out of Rick's house where evidence needed to be recorded. Patti wondered what special rights allowed Erick to request additional officers stay out of his house.

Eventually, Detective Schultz called on the police radio and told the three officers to leave Erick's premises. Shultz ordered Officer Foy and

Patti to remain outside in the sheriff car. Officer Foy did not understand why Schultz was sending the other officers away.

Patti was unaware that Erick had convinced Detective Schultz that she had been living with him. He used the clothes he had taken from her house a day ago. It was Erick's conniving plan all the while, and it worked for his advantage.

Officer Foy and Patti sat in the patrol car and waited for over an hour while Detective Schultz was inside Erick's house. It was an hour past off-duty time for the officer. Detective Schultz finally entered Erick's doorway and handed Patti's purse and clothing to Officer Foy.

With all the evidence: hands cuffed behind her back, tied legs, visible bruises, they did not arrest Erick that day. Patti was sent home in the patrol car. She was stunned, tired, and scared. She felt angry that Detective Schultz and the Prosecutor, Perry Snelling, were unconcerned and insensitive in their response to her physical assault, sexual abuse, and emotional trauma.

It was not until two weeks later that Prosecutor Snelling called Patti to come to his office. He told her that on November 10, 1995, at 1:30 p.m., Erick had been arrested and walked out on a $5,000 bond for the October 26–30, 1995, Criminal, Battery charges.

During the abuse, Erick bragged to Patti that he could do anything and get out on bond and do it again. His statement had just been proven true. Just like that, he was out and free to come after Patti again.

Once again, Patti was unsafe. She was constantly looking over her shoulder. Weary of sounds. She was staying with family and friends.

Patti now understands the *Pattern* in the cycle of domestic violence is a typical cycle revolving from abuse treatment to honeymoon techniques used on victims to conjure a victim into staying in the abusive relationship.[13] Erick was a professional user of the *Pattern* as he had abused his wife Jessie and other women over the years.

Patti was so vulnerable, so blind, so used, so determined to believe in Erick. She was easily taken in by Erick's Pattern.

Patti had prayed, and God heard her prayer. He brought her through to help victims someday. She is a witness to what God has done and prays others will believe He can help them find a safe way out. She wants other victims of abuse to believe in Him.

Remember, in the Bible, God's word tells you He does not want someone to hurt you. God hears your prayers. Here is a blessing of the afflicted when he is overwhelmed and pours out his complaint before the Lord:

Hear my prayer, O Lord, and let my cry come unto thee.

Hide not thy face from me in the day when I am in trouble; incline thine ear unto me: in the day when I call, answer me speedily (Psalm 102:1–2).

14

THE COMMAND AND THE KEY

On December 19, 1995, Erick again found his way to Patti with an evil plan. Erick kidnapped Patti and had Patti dress in his uniform shirt, shoes, pants, and large moon boots that came up to her knees. He taped her elbows and wrists together and took her to his garage. He pushed her down onto the garage floor. He had taped her hands together at the elbows in front so tightly she could hardly breathe. He pushed her down onto the dirty garage floor. Taped and in his boots she could not move.

Patti saw an old, big dirty car up in a car rack, and she panicked when he lowered the lift. She knew she did not want to be put into the trunk of that car. She was horrified, wondering what he planned to do. She could not imagine why he would put her in the car's trunk. Would he put her inside the trunk, raise the lift, and leave her up there? Would he take the car somewhere and set it on fire? She felt faint. He walked to the front of his garage where the customer's car keys were hanging and picked a key off the hanger on the wall.

A fear came over her that she had never experienced before. She began crying and praying to God. Erick was walking back to the car's trunk with the key in his hand when just as he got to the trunk, the key disappeared. It was gone! He turned quickly and looked at Patti and realized she had seen the key disappear! It was gone from his hand! She had seen it happen. He was coming ferociously across the room with unrestrained violence, and Patti knew from the look on his face that he would beat her because she had witnessed this miracle. He was demonic.

Thy word is a lamp unto my feet and a light unto my path (Psalm 119:105).

Patti was holding her breath. She feared for her life. She was on the floor, and Erick was coming across the room. He was mad as if Patti herself had made the key disappear. Patti stiffened, ready for his fist to hit her. Instead, she heard a loud command, *"DELIVER US FROM EVIL!"* It was not her voice. It was not Erick's voice. He stopped dead in his tracks and jumped backward.

Patti was amazed. She could not believe what she had just heard and seen. She had been saved from being trapped inside that old car trunk. God saved her at that moment, and she was in a trance from knowing God was in that old garage with her. She knew the power of God was there in this room. She knew He saved her from Erick's retched plan. What a miracle. She was amazed. Glory to God; He was there with her!

It was beautiful to know that the Almighty God was there with her in the center of her greatest struggle. Faith flourished by showing itself in the conquest. Erick heard the voice too. He just stood in that garage. Patti was wondering what he would do next. She hoped he would let her go, but he was too far into his evil plans to stop.

Erick was agitated and desperate. He pushed Patti into her car and drove toward Indianapolis. Patti did not know what Erick was planning. The snow was ten inches deep. Schools were closed, and absolutely no one was out driving. It was a snow-frozen world with no one around. After driving over icy streets, they reached Indianapolis; Erick stopped and went into a store that looked like a barred-up gun store. He stood looking out the door and had warned her before going in that no one was around to help her, and she was still taped with furnace tape.

Erick came out with a set of handcuffs. Patti was terrified at what he had planned. Erick had been driving blocks in the deep snow when he made another stop behind an old, abandoned Marsh Store. He had stopped to put Patti inside the trunk of her car. Just as he opened the trunk, a semitrailer truck pulled in and the driver was getting out of his truck. As Erick walked to the back of the car, Patti used her tied hands to unlock her door by pushing up the door lock. She knew it would relock automatically at twenty miles per hour. Erick drove out of the parking lot and stopped at the next light. The door was still unlocked. This was the only time to get out of the car; she pushed up on the door handle, opening it.

Patti pushed the door with her right foot and tried but could not get completely out. Erick kept driving and holding on to her at the same time. She was halfway out, and he dragged her a block before he drove into a massive pile of snow at the next block. Patti was almost out, but her taped hands and the enormous work boots had stopped her from getting up. He was across the passenger seat, pulling her back inside. She saw an opening under the steering wheel, and she lunged across the floorboard under the steering wheel and out the driver's door onto the pile of snow.

Three people in a pickup truck had stopped. Patti was elated to see them. They had reported to the Cumberland Metropolitan Police Department that a pedestrian was struck by a car. Immediately, Erick drove off with Patti's car. Patti was screaming, "He stole my car!"

The three people tried to stop him but could not. The Cumberland Metropolitan Police Department (CMPD) came to her aid.

Patti knows this was in God's plans for this to happen just one mile outside Hancock County's authority. She felt His protection and love. If this had happened in Hancock County, she would not have been helped. The incident occurred in Marion County, down the street from the Cumberland Metropolitan Police Department (CMPD) . They sent her in an ambulance to an Indianapolis hospital for X-rays and notified her family. Patti's son, Greg, was at the hospital immediately and took her home. They were highly competent in following up on the charges for

her abduction, battery, and unauthorized use of her vehicle. However, Cumberland PD had an extremely difficult time getting a response from Hancock County Sheriff Department regarding the charges on Gevedon. Hancock County ignored charges on Erick. They commented to Cumberland PD, "They are just having a lover's quarrel, again!"

This was the turning point for Patti. With CMPD handling the case, it was the first time Patti had been treated as a victim. Their concern for her was the first time she had been recognized as a victim needing help in three years. This was disturbing to everyone. The CMPD officer investigating the matter expressed that Erick needed to be caught and punished for the crimes he committed Patti.

A day later when Patti talked with Michael Crooke, Chief of the Cumberland Metropolitan Police Department, she told him how difficult it was to get help from Hancock law enforcement. She believed it was due to the machine guns, silencers, and machine gun shells Erick had in his machine shop. She had seen the guns at his house. He brought a gun and silencer to Patti's home and shot into her lake at the back of her house. She had seen his arsenal of automatic weapons, silencers, and barrels of shells. Hancock knew he had them and feared him.

Chief Crooke immediately contacted the Alcohol, Tobacco, and Firearms (ATF), and they were called in to investigate the automatic weapons and ATF made additional charges. This was grandeur news.

ATF Special Agent Dwight Rapp contacted Patti to handle the case, and after finding an arsenal of automatic guns and silencers, the ATF called in the FBI. The machine guns, automatic guns, and silencers were sent to Washington, D.C., where they were analyzed and found to be handmade, illegal weapons. Charges were filed, and the ATF assigned a Fugitive Task Force to look for Erick. They profiled him on "America's Most Wanted."

Chief Crooke of the CMPD filed charges for abduction, battery, and unauthorized motor vehicle use. These charges were reported to the Marion County Prosecutor, who charged Erick for his abusive, violent, coercive, forceful, threatening treatment and violent attacks.

However, Erick had already convinced officials in Hancock County that what had happened was not an abduction or abuse. HCSD reported to CMPD it was a lover's quarrel and did not charge Erick.

Patti was shocked and didn't understand why Erick had abducted her and dressed her in his clothing. He planned to put her in a car on a car lift in his garage. Why? She did not know until she was told Javedon had a date coming soon in Hancock County Court for the confinement charge when he chained and handcuffed her for three days in October. Erick and his lawyer were claiming Patti had agreed to be handcuffed in a sex act. Erick had planned to use the handcuffs to video Patti in the sex act and present it in the trial.

Patti had prayed, *"Help me, Lord!"* She was a witness to His saving grace. What a blessing. God had arranged for Patti to be rescued in Marion County, just one mile from the Hancock County line. In Marion County, the law went forward and charged Erick with carjacking. God had planned this blessing. Officials in Hancock County were content to say that what had happened in October was not an abduction or abuse; they did not file charges on Erick.

Patti and her son Greg went to the Hancock Sheriff's Department to ask them to retrieve Patti's car from Erick's car lot. But the HCSD officer refused to help with her car. The officer told Patti and Greg that the Sheriff required a county court order to get her car. Even with the fact that Cumberland MPD had notified HCSD of the carjacking and Patti's escape in Cumberland. Patti thought, *"WHY, DO I NEED A COURT ORDER TO GET MY OWN CAR. This man stole my car?"* They were confused and frustrated!

To no avail, Greg and his mother had no recourse but to leave. They needed protection to retrieve Patti's car and they could not get help from HCSD.

The next day Patti asked her attorney friend Candy what to do to get her car. Well, Candy made the call and set up a meeting with a Hancock Sheriff Officer to retrieve the vehicle. Just after work that evening, they headed to the jail and waited an hour for an officer. Then Candy said,

"Let's go get your car. I know by law it is right to get it." "Ok," Patti said. "right but not safe."

She was worried, but her friend insisted. The snow had been coming down for days and was frozen solid.

It was a dark, cold night when they got to Eric's auto repair lot to get her LeBaron. Patti had her extra set of car keys. She gasped when she spotted her car stuck solid in a foot of snow! Suddenly fear came over her. They were here on Erick's car lot all alone! "Are we crazy?" Patti said to Candy. Then Patti thought, *"Yes, but when you have one friend like Candy and God with you, it makes you strong."*

There was no way she would have gone there to get her car except for her friend's encouragement, which gave her the courage to begin taking back her life. Patti knew she wasn't going to get help from the HCSD. Erick had carjacked her car and driven onto his business lot, but the Sheriff would not retrieve her vehicle.

They were in danger on his car lot. They could surely be trapped, or shot, trying to get her car. God had heard her prayers and answered them. It was a miracle. In frozen snow, they retrieved Patti's car from Erick's car lot. Candy's strong spirit, friendship, and care were an encouragement to Patti. Candy and Patti knew they were blessed that night as they sped away.

15

THE MASKED PREDATOR / THE MIRACLE OF THE LOST KEY

Even the spirit of truth; whom the world cannot receive, because it seeth him not, neither knoweth him: but ye know him; for he dwelleth with you and shall be in you (John 14:17).

On January 4, 1996, a winter snowstorm arrived midday, dumping nine inches of snow throughout Indiana. There was a severe weather warning, and the state advised staff to leave early due to the hazardous road condition. Since the thirty-mile trip from the city to her house was over icy, snow-covered roads with extremely slow-moving traffic, Patti decided to get off I-70 interstate. She would take the time to get her nails done at Pro-Nail Shop, thinking the traffic would be lighter later.

Patti was driving a rental car because when Erick carjacked her Chrysler LeBaron convertible, he caused mechanical problems. She took it to the dealership for repairs, and they issued her a rental car while repairs were being made.

Patti is the world's worst at losing keys. When she stopped the rental car and turned it off, she immediately said to herself, "*Don't lose this key!*" She grasped the key tightly so as not to lose it. She started to open the door and noticed the key was not in her hand. How could this be?

Frustrated, she searched everywhere. Patti turned her purse inside and out. She looked on the floorboard and under the seat. She got out of the

71

car and looked in the snow. She could not find the key. She had been so intent on not losing the key that she was now perplexed and annoyed.

Fortunately, the manager of the Pro-Nail Shop came out on his way to pick up sandwiches for the shop attendants when he saw Patti. He stopped to help. He could tell Patti was cold, so he suggested she go into the shop and get her nails done while he looked for the key. She was frantic. How would she get home? It was twenty miles to her house! Nobody would want to come in this blizzard and take her home.

When she got inside the Pro-Nail Shop, frantic, she called her son, Greg, and told him she had just lost her rental car key and asked if he could pick her up and take her home. She was getting her nails done when the manager came in with the key. He said he found it in the snow. Patti was so glad he found the key. She will never understand how that key got in the snow. She did not know how she had lost it. She had been intent in not losing it. Perplexing!

Patti called Greg to tell him the shop manager had found the key and she did not need him to come to take her home. She was heading home now. Greg said, "Mom, please call me when you get home! The roads are so slick. I want to make sure you don't have a slide-off." Patti promised to call him as soon as she got home. She left the Pro-Nail Shop and drove slowly twenty miles over ice and snow on the interstate to her home north of Greenfield.

At approximately 9:30 p.m., Patti arrived home tired from a long day at work and an exhausting icy journey, not to mention the frustration of dealing with the lost key. Patti pulled her car into the garage and opened the door to her foyer. She heard her kitchen wall phone ringing as she disarmed her home alarm. This reminded her that she had promised to call Greg as soon as she arrived home. The icy roads and nine to twelve inches of fallen snow had detained her longer than expected, and Greg was probably worried. She did not take the time to reset her home alarm. Patti ran into the kitchen to answer the phone.

She picked up the phone and said, "Hello? Hello? Greg?" At the same time, she heard heavy running and saw a man running toward her. "Hello?

Hello? Help! HELP!" she yelled into the phone, and the phone went dead. A man wearing a Carhart jacket was running towards her. He was disguised with a ghastly head mask, heavy clothing, gloves, high boots, and chains dangling from the belt around his waist.

Just as she tried to run, she felt the stun gun. He grabbed her and struggled but struck her with the stun gun on the neck. What a stinging, electrical feeling; it was unbearable. She was fighting violently when she hit her head on the kitchen stove and went down to the floor. The man held her there. Half-conscious, she tried to breathe, but the gasoline-soaked glove held tightly over her mouth stopped her attempt. Patti tried to call out, but her scream was stopped. As she struggled to breathe, the man replaced the glove with tape, strapping it over her mouth. Her pounding heartbeat was echoing in her head, and she was feeling faint. Hot tears were streaming down her face as she thought, *"I'm going to die. My God, what is happening?"*

Patti still had her heavy coat on and thought she could struggle to get out from under him, but he was too heavy. He was now sitting on her, rolled her over onto her face, and pulled her coat off. He chained her hands behind her. His weight was smothering. He taped her mouth; breathing was even more complicated. He used the chains dangling from his belt to chain her legs. Then he began dragging her across the floor. Patti knew she would die, and no one would know she was missing for days, especially in this snowstorm since the roads were becoming hazardous.

Tightly bound and gagged, he rolled and dragged her down the three stairs in the living room and across her foyer. He continued dragging her out into the garage. As she resisted, he pulled her hair, hit her, and gouged her with the stun gun on the back and neck. He dropped her down and stood on her with his boots as he tried to get the keys out of the ignition. She tried to resist, but her body was too sluggish. How ironic. Erick was putting her into her rental car Patti had rented because he had car-jacked her LeBaron just two weeks earlier in November 1995, when Patti was rescued by the Cumberland Metropolitan Police Department in Marion County. They reported the carjacking crime to Hancock County

Sheriff's Department and told them Erick still had possession of Patti's car. The HCSD department refused to retrieve Patti's car from Erick's car lot. Erick had kept Patti's car, and now he was putting her into the car she had rented!

There was a glimmer of hope as she remembered she had dropped the keys to her rental into the opening between the car seats. This was a habit that had become part of her defense with the kind of torture she had suffered at Erick's hands for the last four years. But she knew her attacker all too well. She had been fighting the truth. She knew that this attacker was not someone new. She knew Erick was behind the ghastly mask, and there was no hope of escape this time.

As he ravaged the car for the keys, she felt hopeless as he found them and opened the car's trunk. No words could come from her mouth, but her thoughts pounded in her head, *"No! I'm claustrophobic!"* She was already smothered and choking. She thought, *"Do not let this man put me in the trunk, please God!"*

Fear paralyzed Patti's body, mind, and spirit as he closed the trunk. She heard the garage door go up and felt the car start. The car began to move, and the garage door closed. The sound of the tires going over the snow echoed in Patti's ears, and she thought she could tell which way the car was turning as it left out of the driveway.

In total darkness, breathing in the smell of the trunk, bound with belts around her feet and with her hands tied behind her back, Patti's mind was frozen with overwhelming fear. "I am going to die," she thought. The moment the trunk lid closed, Patti knew she would die. The trunk was icy cold. Patti was wearing only a sweater and slacks and had no coat or shoes. Even though she felt her fate was already sealed, she had to fight. She had to try. She had to think about how to free herself from these chains. She thought maybe if she could get out of the chains and belts, she could hit him with the tire tools when he opened the trunk. This gave her hope.

The trunk was dark and small. Patti began to curl up, and she rolled her knees toward her stomach, which allowed her to pull her arms under her rear and wiggle her hands under her buttocks to pull them around her feet and in front of her. It seemed like that took forever, but time was the only thing Patti had. She struggled and finally got enough room to get her hands out of the chain. Then she tore the tape from her mouth and worked to get free of the belt on her feet and waist.... It worked!

Her senses told her to leave evidence inside the trunk, so she took her earrings off and put them in the spare tire compartment. Patti pulled out some small strands of hair and tucked them wherever she could to find a place where this evil predator would not see them. He was always very skillful in covering his wickedness. He possessed expert knowledge in the game of his Reign of Terror. He was a demon, inflicting almost unimaginable human suffering.

As Erick was driving, he yelled at the top of his voice with rage. He told her he would stop the car and kill her if she made noise. Patti worked on ankle straps around her ankles for some time before she got them off. This took time, but she was determined.

Patti put her fingerprints over the trunk in all the holes she could touch. She tried to get the tire out of the tire hole to get to the jack. She thought she could hit Erick with it when he opened the trunk, but she also knew that would be exceedingly difficult because she would be below him, and if she didn't get the chance to hit him hard enough, he would kill her.

Patti pleaded with Erick while inside the trunk to please let her out. He was yelling back questions about the incident on December 19 when he had carjacked her, and she escaped to Marion County. He wanted to know if the Cumberland Police Department kept the clothing he had disguised her in two weeks earlier. Also, he wanted to know what she reported to the Hancock Sheriff about the December incident. She told him the carjacking was written by the Cumberland Metropolitan Police Department (CMPD) in Marion County. The Marion County prosecutor already had the evidence and charged him with kidnapping.

Patti did not tell him that she had disclosed her concern about the machine guns, silencers, and explosives Erick had in his house and garage to the CMPD or that they immediately contacted the Alcohol Tobacco and Firearms (ATF) and the Federal Bureau of Investigations (FBI).

The ATF is a primary law enforcement agency for the U.S. government, charged with enforcing more than 200 categories of federal laws; the ATF primarily enforces federal firearms statutes and investigates arson and bombings.[14]

He didn't know she had talked with the ATF and they had begun investigating him. Knowing that she had told the ATF of his weapons was a relief. If something happened and she was missing, the ATF would become involved. She only hoped the ATF would look for her. But the reality was she needed help now. He was furiously yelling that he would ensure that she would never testify in either case against him. She knew she was going to die.

After what seemed to Patti to be all night long, Erick stopped the car and started talking to someone. Patti thought that if she could get that someone's attention, they would call the police. Patti was so excited when she heard voices. She began screaming and pounding and kicking in the trunk. Her heart was beating so fast that she thought she might be helped soon.

Patti knew Erick thrived on maltreatment and causing intense fear. She must not let his physical, psychological, and sexual abuse control her now. Patti knew this had become a struggle between good and evil, and God was her victor. She prayed! Patti called upon the Lord in her distress and cried unto her God: *"He heard her voice out of his temple, and her cry came before him, even unto his ears" (Psalm 18:1–6)*.

Patti held her right hand up as high as she could in the trunk and prayed, "God, I know I will die, and that is alright. I am ready to go to heaven!" At that moment, Patti was not cold or scared anymore. A soothing peace beyond any she had ever known took over. Patti knew God was there in that trunk with her. A verse of scripture came to her mind, *"PEACE I leave with you, my peace I give unto you: not as the world giveth, give I unto you" (John 14:27)*. Immediately, sadness flooded over her as she thought how horrible it would be for her family. They would be so torn up. They would be so hurt and grieve so much. They may never find her body. This was going to destroy them.

Patti prayed again, "God, please let the truth come out about this evil man." Another verse came to her mind, "*Let not your heart be troubled, neither let it be afraid" (John 14:27)*. She spoke words to her mother, even though she wasn't there. She said, "Mom, know that I did everything possible to get away. Do not worry; I am at peace."

Patti would later learn that on that very night, her mother was asleep but was awakened when she heard Patti's voice. She got out of bed and walked into her kitchen, looking for Patti. Patti's mother heard her voice say, "Mom, know that I did everything possible to get away. Do not worry; I am at peace." Of course, Patti was not at her mother's home, she was tied up in the car's trunk, but God had a plan for her.

Erick's voice cut into her thoughts and prayers, "I guess you thought you would be heard by someone who cared! He did not care when he heard you." Erick was referring to the male voice that she heard. The voice she heard was not a source of help but was instead the voice of someone assisting Erick with the kidnapping. She was disillusioned and lost all hope at that moment. Erick continued driving and yelling at her. Then, finally, hours later, he stopped the car. She thought he would kill her and bury her in this isolated place in the dark night.

Oh, God, please help, she thought. She was terrified.

Erick got her out of the trunk and brought her to the front seat. He handcuffed her left wrist and pushed her head under the steering wheel. He handcuffed her right hand to the bar under the passenger seat, then kept driving. As they continued driving, this predator jabbed his stun gun on her as he asked her questions regarding the December carjacking incident. Also, he wanted to know about his blue bathrobe she had on during the October 1995 kidnapping. She told him, "The Hancock Sheriff Department took the housecoat and the handcuffs for evidence."

Patti could look up from under the steering wheel and see the overhead interstate I-74 sign, and thought they were near Ohio.

After driving around for hours, he received a call on his cellular phone, and he told someone, "Meet us at the last place we stopped at and bring the Jose Cuervo and Sprite." Soon after the call, Erick stopped the car again and rolled down his window. With her head under the steering wheel, Patti could see a man's hands in the window holding bottles of Jose Cuervo and Sprite. Erick started forcing her to drink Jose Cuervo. He pushed her into the dashboard and jerked her head back and forth if Patti wouldn't drink. All the time, he was hitting her with the stun gun and his fists and pulling her hair. Sometimes he would stop and urinate out by the car.

After drinking some of that Jose Cuervo, Patti vomited on the car and herself. He got even angrier and made her drink again and again. Then he called someone on his cell phone and told them, "Go to my garage and get ready and wait for us to come there." Patti couldn't believe another human was helping this mad man do this to her. Why? Patti wondered why Erick was forcing her to drink Jose Cuervo. Why? As time passed, Patti discovered Erick had a dreadful, repellent, ghastly plan to video a sexual act with her in handcuffs to indicate she had been in a sexual act when she escaped from his house on October 30. She didn't know how he would carry out his macabre, sick plan.

As Erick and the man were talking on the phone, Patti heard Erick say, "Man, I know it's taking longer than we planned, but it won't take too much longer."

Then, Erick gave his accomplice more instructions. He said, "Man when I drive back to the garage, open the overhead garage door. But keep hidden in the little garage until I get her in the house, then close the garage door."

He said in a stronger voice, "Man, this is a rental car. Clean it inside and out. Scrub it all over and get the trunk good. Look for things she might have put in here. Get rid of all of her hair, anything. She took the whole trunk apart, check under the spare tire, and put it in place."

When he pulled inside his garage, reality hit her, and Patti panicked and began to cry. She could only pray that this person helping Erick would hear her and help, but she knew there was no help. She wondered, *"Why would any person be a part of hurting her? Why would they help Erick?"*

The air was bitter cold, and the ground was covered with snow. Erick made her take off all her clothes in the car. He put them in the back seat next to her hat and gloves. He twisted her arm, pulled her hair, and made her walk fast from his garage across the parking lot toward the back door of his house. Walking barefoot and without clothing, Patti looked at the full moon, bright stars, and moonlight shining on the snow. A little breeze softly touched her, and she knew she was alive. Patti prayed and felt the presence of God nearby.

Erick unlocked the door and pushed her inside! When he got her inside his house, he told Patti, "You are going to make a sex video wearing these handcuffs." He took the handcuffs out of the bag and said, " You are going to ask me for these handcuffs to be put on while we are having sex." Then he warned her violently, "You need to be convincing if you want to live."

She said, "No!" "I will not do that!" He became violent! He twisted her arms, hit her, then pulled her hair. She said, "No!" again. He threatened her and said, "Do you want to die"?

Erick had planned a script for this video. He became more violent. There was no way out, and Patti had to comply and ask him to put handcuffs on her wrists. To make this look realistic, he said you will talk about Beth, your boss. He called from his cellular phone to make his home phone line ring, and Patti was to pretend the next-door neighbor, Peggy, was calling Erick. Patti was to get angry. The plot was for her to act as if she was furious and jealous of Peggy.

Erick had planned this reenactment to say it was a video from October 1995 when Patti escaped from Erick's house with handcuffs on her wrists and pantyhose tied around her feet, wearing Erick's blue bathrobe—except he did not have the blue bathrobe for the video. The Hancock Sheriff had it.

This enactment would make the October 1995 incident look as if Patti willingly had handcuffs on while having sex with Erick. He said the police would think Patti was involved in a sex act and something went wrong, so Patti got up and ran out of his house down U.S. 40 wearing his bathrobe.

He would present this in county court, and all charges would be dropped on the October 1995 confinement and battery.-10

While inside the Myer's store, Erick told Patti that the clothes he had purposely taken from her house he would keep at his house as a ploy to prove to the sheriff's department she was staying with him. He laughed because they believed him. He had outsmarted them again. He was playing his game, preying on people, and outwitting the law.

Erick told her during the discussion with Detective Sullivan, he told Sullivan, that Patti was at his house and wanted to have sex with handcuffs. Erick even showed Sullivan her clothes to prove she was staying with him. He was so conniving and convincing! Erick had created a misconception that caused law enforcement to believe him. He had made sure they were seen together in public, had her clothes at his house, misled the detective, and now he was making her do this video as proof for his court date. He was filled with evil.

Patti repeatedly told him, "No!" She would not make the video. Then he said he could easily poison her family's food while grocery shopping. He would inject it into their hamburger meat. "It will be your fault when they all die of food poisoning," he said. Overwhelming fear froze her heart. She had no choice. She could not risk him hurting her family.

Erick continued with his plan. He forced her to act out his story with the handcuffs while he videoed it. It was a forced sexual act frightful, ter- rifying, dreadful, ghastly, appalling, repellent, macabre, sick! He recorded the video over and over to get it the way he wanted. This went on for hours all night until late into Friday morning. Patti was abused! Patti feared for her life.

Patti realized they would believe Erick and not her. He had planned to kill Patti and then use the video as evidence for the upcoming trial. Erick could not take the chance of getting caught again. He said he would do whatever to keep his business and stay out of jail. He would be free of any charges when he showed the video. He had written the perfect script. The court would hear his telephone ring and watch Patti answer it. They would see her upset at Peggy next door and hear her accuse Peggy of

being with Erick. They would watch her willingly be handcuffed, nude, and having sex with him. They would see the smeared black makeup on her face that Erick forced her to apply to appear just as she was when she escaped running down U.S. 40 handcuffed in October. He had devised an exact replica of the October abduction, confinement and rape. No one would know that she was forced to make this horrible video. She would not be in court. She would be missing because Erick was going to kill her. And he said they would never even think of looking on his mom's property in southern Indiana. Why would they even connect him to Patti missing?

His trial was just over a week away, and he would be free when he presented this video in court. He would be cleared of all charges. She prayed to God! He gave her help while this horrible abduction and abuse were going on; Patti was not aware that anyone was looking for her.

When Patti did not call Greg to say she was safely home after her snowy drive from the nail salon, Greg had called her house. Patti did not answer! He called the Hancock Sheriff's Department and asked them to check if she made it home through the snow. A deputy went to her house, and she wasn't there. They could not locate Patti. They called Greg and her daughter, Ramona, to let them know Patti was not home. Greg and Ramona began to fear something awful had happened to their mother. They knew of her issues with Erick.

Right-a-way, they got to her house and found definite signs of men's boot tracks in the snow around the back and side of her home that led into her garage. They noticed her car had left traces in the snow going into her garage and coming out again and back down the driveway. The falling snow would have covered these boot tracks and car tracks if they were from the morning.

They searched inside her house for any clues as to why she wasn't home. Greg knew she promised she would call to let him know when she got to her house after she left the nail salon, but they found no sign of her. They began to fear that something awful had happened. Had Erick done something? Had he abducted their mother? They feared the worst. They looked for more signs and searched the night with no luck.

They continued their search early the following day at Erick's car lot. They did not see their mother's car in his car lot. Suddenly Ramona remembered her mother had a rental car. Erick had kept her car when she escaped in Cumberland, IN. She looked inside cars, and there inside a vehicle, Ramona recognized Patti's clothes piled in the back seat. She saw her coat and boots and knew that ridiculous hat she wore was her mother's. Ramona called the Hancock County Sheriff's Department and told Deputy Mike Smuth that her mom's rental car was in Erick's parking lot at the back of his house. She could see inside the vehicle and saw her mom's clothes, boots, and hat. Ramona and Greg met with Hancock Deputy Smuth and told him about finding their mother's clothing in the rental car. Deputy Smuth finally came to Erick's house, but he refused to knock on Erick's door to look inside the house. Deputy Smuth was uncooperative and left.

Ramona and Greg continued driving around Erick's house and parking lot that day and night. Erick knew they were out in his parking lot, making him extremely nervous.

Although Patti could tell how desperately cunning and determined he seemed she did not know her children were there. He was putting his evil plan into action. He pushed her into the living room and seated her on a chair. He had a gun in his hand. She was in shock and felt like she was ready to pass out. He was not human. He was an evil, demonic predator. She was praying to God. She wanted to see her family again. She knew they would grieve. Then, Erick asked her to hold his handgun. Never would she do that. What was his plan? She was trying to get her mind to work. *Was this going to be a murder-suicide or an effort to get her fingerprints on the gun? He is sadistic*, she thought. She said," NO, I will not hold your gun!" She was determined, exhausted, and in shock. Erick was so callous now. He was inhuman.

He pushed her back into his bedroom. She sat on the side of the waterbed. She wondered what horrible plan he had in mind now. Then he told her, "You have to make a call to Ramona. You will convince her that we are together, happy, and making up. Things are really good now. You want to be with me because you love me. Tell her we are at Lake Monroe on the houseboat. You would have called sooner, but cell phone signals are not good here at the lake." Then he said in a gruff voice, "I will be listening to every word you say." He was standing over her and threatening her. She knew she was in danger. What would he do next?

Patti knew she had to be skillful and weigh alternatives on making the call. She began to think through how to make the call to Ramona. Erick was in her face now. Then he told her, "You have to make a call to Ramona." He would be able to hear her daughter talking, so Patti pressed the cell phone to secure into her ear. While Erick was talking, Patti slowly slid into the large pillows on the waterbed and braced her neck and head for protection from his hands. She knew Ramona would be sound asleep, and Patti needed to have her alert at the beginning of the call. Patti thought about her new granddaughter, Elizabeth, who was only a few months old. That was it, thought Patti, *the baby*!

Then, waving the gun, Erick told her, "You have to make a call to Ramona now." Patti called, and after a few rings, Ramona answered. Patti did not say "hello"; instead, she said in a pleading voice, "WHY IS THE BABY CRYING? IS SHE SICK? WHAT IS WRONG?" Patti was praying her daughter was awake and alert. Now! Ramona said, "MOM, WHERE ARE YOU?"

Those were just the words Patti desperately needed her to say! Patti's reply was, "ERICK'S! HELP!" Instantly, Erick slammed the cell phone closed very hard! X-rays would later show he'd closed the cell phone so hard that it broke her little finger on her right hand. Erick didn't take the time to hit her. He threw Patti's keys at her. She ran out the door, got in her car, and drove ninety miles per hour out of his parking lot onto U.S. 40, Main Street in Greenfield. She drove past the Hancock County Jail just as fast. She knew they would not help. She wasn't stopping at 3:00 a.m. Everything was closed. Finally, she saw an open gas station. She skidded into the parking lot and jumped out of her car, running into the station and screaming, "HELP!" "HELP!"

Just as she got inside the door, an HCSD patrol car pulled into the gas station parking lot, and right behind the patrol car was Patti's daughter driving in, screaming to the officers that her mom had been missing and Erick Javedon had kidnapped her from her home. Ramona had called the Sheriff, and she had come to rescue Patti. Her daughter had rescued her. She would have been dead. In two weeks, the videos would have set Erick William Javedon free of any charges in court.

The turn off the interstate in the snowstorm and losing the *key* was a "miracle"! God had planned for her to lose her *key*. The *key* was her call for help. It was her alarm to Greg. If she had not lost the *key*, she would not have called Greg, and he would not have been waiting for her to call. No one would have known Erick had kidnapped Patti if not for the lost *key*. He would kill her after he had the video. God used the *key* as the help signal to her children. Patti knew this was God's plan. She could not contain all this miracle of the key. It was surreal what had happened because of the key. She did not lose it. God had it all the while she was frustrated looking for it. Patti knew she will glorify God! *"I will deliver thee, and thou shalt glorify me."* (Psalm 50:15)-KJV.

Patti was convinced that Erick was so filled with satanic desires that God fought him and protected her. It was evil against God, and God had won the battle every time, and Patti survived time and time again. God saved Patti, and He surrounded her with angels-KJV-4. She was a witness to show God's love and power and what He can do for you.

On January 29, three weeks later, Detective John Munden informed Patti Hancock County Sheriff had tracked Erick Javedon to a hotel in Seymour, IN where he had been staying for three days. As they pulled into the parking lot, he'd escaped from his room. They confiscated his car and found evidence; he had purchased a laptop, written a twelve-page document about her, and made forty-three copies of the pornographic rape video he had forced her to act out. Before he got caught while in the southern Indiana town of North Vernon, he had made thirty-eight copies of the sex tape. HCSD confiscated the forty-three sex tapes, his computer, video camera, and a twelve-page letter about Patti. There did not seem to

be an end to his reign of terror. Patti would have been dead, consequently, the videos would have set Erick William Javedon free of all charges in court in two weeks. But God was in control and Patti remained safe.

Erick escaped and immediately went on the run again. Patti continued receiving threatening calls from Erick, saying he knew where she was. He may have been on the run, but he continued calling and was still bringing terror into her life. The reports in the newspaper said he had been seen around Hancock County. He eluded capture for nearly a year.

16

HEADLINES - ATF MOST WANTED CAUGHT

After being on the run for nearly a year, the ATF caught Erick William Javedon on October 3, 1996, in Florence, KY. A division of the ATF, the Alcohol, Tobacco, and Firearms-4 Special Agent, Dwight Rapp, called Patti at work around 1 pm to notify her that Erick had been picked up on a traffic violation. Finally, at last, Patti thought almost ten months after her previous abduction, the ATF had caught him. He was arrested!

Patti remembers she felt faint! A rush of blood went through her body that jolted her whole being. She was so emotional. Just natural streams of water flowed silently from her eyes. Not sobs! Patti was overwhelmed with feelings of relief and joy!

Patti had fought for her life for years! A rush of memories grasped her mind. Memories of violence, being abducted, being held captive, and living in fear every second since that horrible day on January 4th, 1996, when he abducted her from her home. She feared for all her family for almost a year. Everyone had been on edge and fearful since he had been on the run. There were reports of sightings of him in the county, and no one could relax until he was caught.

Now she would be safe. And more importantly, her mother, son, daughter, and grandchildren would be safe. Now, justice would be served...or so she thought!

The Alcohol, Tobacco, and Firearms-4 Special Agent Dwight Rapp indicated it would be around two weeks before he was returned to Indiana. Erick would be incarcerated in the Marion County Jail and moved to a federal prison out of state until the trial.

17

FEDERAL TRIAL

The wait for the federal trial was a torturous two long years. Although Patti was in the Federal Victims Protection Program, she was sometimes uneasy. She never knew who was sent to protect her or who was paid and sent by Erick to harm her. Patti began to get nervous and was suspicious of everyone. She knew she could not live so frightened, always looking over her shoulder, not knowing who would harm her. Patti prayed to God to protect her and to let her know when she would be in danger.

She remembered a scripture, "*Peace I leave with you peace I give to you; not as the world gives do I give to you. Let not your heart be troubled, neither let it be afraid" (John 14:27)*. And that very day Patti felt a peace cover over her that settled deep in her heart.

The time had come. It was the first day of the dreaded federal trial, held in Room 105 of the Birch Bayh Federal Building and the United States Courthouse in Indianapolis, Indiana.

The Alcohol, Tobacco, Firearms (ATF) division under the Federal Bureau of Investigation issues firearms licenses and conducts firearms licensee qualification and compliance.[15] Their inspection and investigations of Erick Wiliam Javedon for possessing and manufacturing firearms and other criminal violations resulted in federal charges. Patti was the critical witness testifying for the Federal Government in the court case against Javedon. She had seen the automatic weapons at his residence and had once witnessed him shooting into an old car at his mother's home. He bought a large quantity of ammunition loaded into his vehicle from a farm wagon. On a couple of occasions, he had shotguns from her patio door using a homemade silencer.

Patti had been so nervous and restless, sleeping little the night before. Getting dressed, she wished she had agreed to her son or daughter staying the night with her for comfort and support, but they both had small children, and she didn't want to bother them. Patti assured them she should be fine testifying in court as a witness against this evil man to the illegal weapons for the U.S. Government.

That morning, when Patti started her car, it sputtered, and she immediately smelled gas fumes as she backed out of her garage and driveway. She immediately knew something wasn't right. Just a mile down the road, Patti knew there was a problem when the car sputtered and stopped on State Road 9, just a short distance from the Monroe Car Repair Shop. She wondered if Erick might have hired someone to put something into her car gas tank.

When the car stopped, she said a prayer. *This can't be happening!* Paralyzed with fear and emotionally drained, Patti ran into the Monroe Auto Repair Shop. She was frantic. It was a moment before she realized Sheriff Gulling was standing in the shop. What a blessing he was there, right at the shop where she pulled in for help.

The Sheriff asked Patti what was wrong. She told him, "My car smells like gasoline and stopped running. I think someone is making sure I don't get to the Federal Court House to testify against Erick Javedon."

Of course, Sheriff Gulling knew well about the federal trial, just as everyone in the county knew. The repair shop was full of local men discussing Erick's federal trial. This was a blessing that God had provided a safe place for her to get help. Praise to the Lord. He had! What a miracle. Miraculously, the sheriff provided an officer to escort Patti into Indianapolis, where the federal trial was being held. She felt secure as she stepped out of the sheriff's car in front of the Birch Bayh Federal Building/ the United States Courthouse. Patti remembered the Scripture,

"I am with you and will watch over you wherever you go!"
(Gen. 28:15).

Patti knew God had provided the police escort. Her fear had sub-sided. How could it be explained that Sheriff Gulling just happened to be there for her? It was beyond understanding. Divine! She would not have gotten to the federal trial without his help. God had rescued her again. Once inside the courthouse, Patti met with the witness protection liaison, Vicki. She had protected Patti since Erick had been federally charged in 1996. Vickie had assured her she would be held alone in a secure room during the trial.

The interior of the federal courthouse was very elaborate, with marble floors, suspended chandeliers, massive pillars, oak paneling, and stained windows. Patti was directed upstairs and down a long hall past a court-room to a witness room. As she walked into the room, her heart skipped a beat; this room was packed with Hancock County Sheriff's Deputies HCSD. Patti believed she was to be in a separate victim's protection room. She was very uncomfortable in the room with them. Some officers had been Erick's allies because they had purchased illegal firearms and silencers from him. He had terrorized some. It had been challenging to get protec-tion from the officers due to their collaboration with Erick. The HCSD had ignored her abuse claims and called her his "girlfriend." Some wit-nesses were the officers who did not help her because they blamed her for what Erick did to her. They referred to Patti as his "girlfriend"! They would not protect her from Erick's violent abuse. After the Cumberland carjacking, Erick fled with her LaBaron and kept it on his Auto and Truck Repair parking lot. Patti asked the HCSD to escort her and friend Candy to retrieve her car from Erick's car lot. They refused to escort help her. They told her to get a court release from the judge.

When Patti had paid $100 for a protection order and hide in the Julian Women's Shelter she gave her neighbor, Effie, a copy of the pro-tection order. A few days later, Effie witnessed Erick breaking into Patti's house and called the Sheriff's Department to report Erick's break-in.

Deputy Smuth came to Patti's house and told Effie the protection paper did not mean anything. Then he just drove away. Patti's home was vandalized with extensive damages that night while she was in the women's and children's shelter.

In addition, Erick had gone to extremes to convince the law enforcement and county court judges that their relationship was mutual. This was another misconception which prevented her from getting help or protection from the law. In all the many *Greenfield Daily Reporter* newspaper articles, the HCSD referred to Patti as Erick's "girlfriend." This was a contradiction to the truth. The relationship was based solely upon his fatal attraction for Patti, and it was that which became her struggle to escape the years she had been kidnaped, chained, beaten, sexually assaulted, and controlled by his evil culpability.

So, why did she live through these horrid things? Patti lived because God loved her and protected her. And even in it all, Patti learned to have faith and trust in God. That faith was her real blessing from God. As the oldest of five she became the one who took care of her siblings, became strong and thought she didn't need any help. She was independent! Until she needed God's blessings.

> *You are much more valuable than the fowls of the air which*
> *He provides for each day. Would He not make provisions*
> *for you? Are you not much better than the fowls of the air?*
> *(Hebrews 11:36–37).*

While Patti was sitting in the witness room listening to their conversations, one deputy looked at her and started a conversation about an incident involving her and Erick. She began feeling extremely uncomfortable with their evasive conversation. She felt infringed upon in this room with them.

At that moment, the reality of the trial and facing Erick was unbearable. She did *not* feel comfortable in this room. Memories flooded Patti's mind, and overwhelming fear came over her.

She had tried to escape from this evil man. Patti suffered at his hands and was beaten, held captive, and raped. Her home was vandalized, and her family was threatened and endangered. Patti remembered the six months away from her home that she spent hiding in a shelter for battered women and children, all the time being stalked by Erick and the men he had hired to hunt her down. She was stalked while she worked. She stayed with a different family member or friend each night for months. It was exhausting. She missed her house and her family. Now she was here and uncomfortable. In addition, Erick had gone to extremes to convince the law enforcement and county court judges that they were in a sexual relationship and it was mutual.

Memories of Erick's wife, Jessie, and the hired men who stalked Patti and were involved in a kidnapping plan to kill her flooded her mind. Erick's ex-wife, Jessie, had confessed to Patti she was involved in vandalizing her home. The fact that no one helped her reminded Patti that this room was filled with people who doubted the truth of what had happened to her. Erick had gone to extremes to convince the law enforcement and county court judges that their relationship was mutual.

Erick had terrorized Patti, her mother, her children, her grandchildren, her neighbors, her co-workers, and her friends. Now his terror continued in her memories and of the people in this room he had convinced with his lies.

Never in her life had Patti ever given up or walked away from anything. Now, she decided she was leaving. Patti knew she could not go through this trial. She could not testify and become his target again. She had never had protection before and didn't expect it now.

Patti had been independent and fearless all her life—strong-willed, emotionally resilient—and able to deal with stress, grief, loss, and other difficulties until Erick's reign of terror ruled her life for years.

She got up and walked out of the witness room. She just walked out.

Faster and faster, she went down the long, elaborate hall with marble floors, suspended chandeliers, massive pillars, and oak paneling. As Patti walked closer to the federal courtroom, she noticed a long, narrow window in the hall. She stopped walking and stood still for a moment.

What should she do?

18

PRAYING FOR COURAGE–GOD SENT ANGELS!

A s Patti stood there, she thought that if she could look into the window of the courtroom and see Erick, maybe she could become strong enough to stay and testify in court against him. Maybe seeing him would strengthen her resolve. She looked into a narrow window.

Her heart skipped a beat. She did not see Erick, but she saw a blessing from God sitting on a bench in the back of the United States Court room. She said, "Thank you, Lord!"

It was Carolyn, her angel, a dear special friend from the Environmental Protection Agency, where they worked together at the Indiana Government Center. Carolyn was the Executive Administrator for the Commissioner of the agency. She rarely had time away from her management duties as she was indispensable to the needs of the Commissioner's Office. Carolyn did not see Patti, but Patti knew that she could not leave now. As she stood there, Patti realized her fear was gone. She had peace and strength at that moment. God had sent Carolyn to give Patti peace.

Carolyn's thoughtfulness and loyalty showed Patti the faith she had in her. Carolyn's caring was not out of obligation but out of the goodness of her heart! Patti knew that the strength she found to survive that long, torturous week would be due to her friend.

This gave Patti a lasting sense of divine peace, tranquility, and harmony. At that moment, Patti found a wall of faith that gave her peace. She did not leave. She continued walking to the end of the long hall and entered the door to the lady's room.

As Patti opened the tall doors into the large, luxurious facility, she heard singing. A well-dressed African American attendant came toward her. She was looking up, singing, smiling, and waving her arms. The attendant said she was praising God, "Oh Jesus, you have five angels-KJV, all around you!" Patti knew God was with her there in this room. She truly *felt* renewed peace, strength, courage, and faith. What an amazing feeling knowing God was there, showing His love and care. Patti's heart was suddenly filled with joy, and tears flowed from her eyes.

Patti had a long talk with the attendant and told her she had planned to leave the federal court room because she had become overwhelmed with fear. But on her way out, God had shown her an angel, her friend Carolyn, sitting all alone in the courtroom, and that seeing this had given her the strength and courage to stay and be a witness against this evil predator. Just now, again, God had surrounded her with angels-KJV. She thought, "five angels-4!" Then she thought *Carolyn was the sixth angel-4*.

Carolyn supported Patti staying the week during the trial and having lunch with her daily. She was a blessing sent by God.

The week-long trial felt more like a year-long trial. Patti's emotions were raw. The Federal Judge Fugate had allowed Erick to represent himself as his lawyer in his trial. Erick took delight in this position. Acting as his attorney, Erick called Patti to testify the first day of the trial. During Patti's testimony, he stood excessively close to her while interrogating and humiliating her. Judge Fugate repeatedly warned him not to get within three feet of her, but Erick continued to intimidate Patti with his new found authority.

After statements Erick made, fortunately, the Judge allowed Patti to enter his history of brutality and his kidnapping charges. At this time, the jury were requested to leave the room before further discussion. Patti discussed Erick's abuse in detail which was heard by those in the courtroom.

Of course, Erick had Patti to testify the first day then he requested her held in the witness room all week as a witness on recall. So, ultimately, Erick deliberately arranged to have her secluded in the witness room the entire week. She was the last witness to testify on the last day of the trial. But each day, God's love evolved around her. "*I am with you and will watch over you wherever you go*" (Genesis 28:15).

Forced to sit in the witness room, the memories of his rapacious and outrageous assaults on her were too much, but Patti kept believing that he would be tried in Hancock Court for the violent destruction and outrageous assaults on her.

Finally, it was over, and the verdict was guilty of multiple violations of law relating to illegal firearms.

19

THE FEDERAL
SENTENCING—VINDICATION

The wait for the sentencing took weeks. The question that everyone was asking was, "Would Patti testify at his sentencing?" But, for her, there was no doubt that she would. The fact that Erick was guilty of possessing and manufacturing illegal firearms, in reality, never made him look as harmful, evil or as dangerous as he was. The terrible abuse he had inflicted upon Patti for so long was what truly made him dangerous.

At his trial sentencing, the federal courtroom was packed with some forty friends and family members of Erick's. Patti did testify, and Erick was given additional time to be served because she testified about his horrible abductions and violent abuse over four years. After her testimony at Eric's sentencing, Judge Fugate stated that he admired Patti for her testimony.

The Judge recommended that when Hancock County tried Erick for the crimes he committed against her, he should get full punishment for the violent destruction and outrageous assaults. He said, "Erick's level of criminal knowledge and culpability should be the law's primary consideration for having a trial." Vindication that day was those family and friends who came to the sentencing heard about his rapacious actions against Patti, Jessi, and other women.

Patti was so humbled by Judge Fugate's words to her that day. Little did Patti know that those would be her first and last good words about justice for her. She experienced the hopes of bringing Erick to trial in Hancock County fade.

20

JUDGE DECIDED NO COUNTY TRIAL

Hancock County Judge Snelling reported to the *Greenfield Daily Reporter* newspaper that after Javedon's federal time for illegal firearms violations was completed, he would proceed with the Hancock County trial for the pending charges on Erick for two kidnappings, abduction, criminal confinement, car theft, invasion of privacy, battery, and unauthorized use of a vehicle which spanned over four years from 1992 to 1996.

While Javedon was serving his federal time in prison, in 2003, God sent a loving Christian husband, Gary into Patti's life. He showered her with genuine love and companionship. His compassion helped Patti in her long healing process.

In 2005, after Erick's prison term was up, the Hancock County Judge Snelling decided he would not have Erick's trial.

Patti, husband Gary, children and the residents of Hancock County were extremely disappointed with Judge Snelling's decision not to hold a trial on the pending Hancock County kidnapping charges against Javedon. Patti had several conversations with Judge Snelling as to why he decided he would not bring Eric to trial. The conversations ended without resolve.

21

NEW PROSECUTOR OPENED THE COLD CASE AND ASSIGNED DETECTIVE JOHN MUNDEN

In 2004, the news about the trial in Hancock County had reached Erick in the U.S. Federal Prison in Texas. The *Greenfield Daily Reporter* newspaper printed articles about Erick's threats while in prison to the newly elected Hancock County Prosecutor, Larry Gossett, and Detective John Munden.

The Hancock County Prosecutor installed $17,000 of safety improvements to his office. They knew Erick would be released from the U.S. Federal Prison in February 2005. Everyone feared for Patti and her family's safety.

There was a welcome development when the newly elected Hancock County Prosecutor, Larry Gossett, opened the "cold case of Erick William Javedon" and assigned Detective John W. Munden to investigate the charges of Kidnapping, Abduction, Criminal Confinement, Car Theft, Exception to Misdemeanor for Invasion of Privacy, Battery, and Unauthorized Use of Vehicle that spanned over four years from 1992 to 1996.

Detective Munden started diligently investigating Erick's charges. He frequently met with Patti, Gary, her husband, her son Greg, and her daughter Ramona to review the case. Patti, Gary and the family all were grateful for Detective Munden's dedication to the investigation of the charges and how he showed care and conscientiousness to seek justice for the crimes Erick had done to Patti.

In 2005, the day came that Erick was released from prison; Prosecutor Larry Gossett had Erick William Javedon arrested at the entrance to the Federal Prison in Texas. He was placed on a one million dollar bond and held in Hancock County Jail until his trial.

Prosecutor Gossett and Detective John Munden knew the evidence guaranteed the conviction for kidnapping, rape, and a multitude of other charges.

Detective John Munden's investigation was thorough and complete. The proof was in the photo of Patti unwrapping the makeup bag on Christmas Eve, 1995. The photo proved the sex video was recorded after Christmas when Erick kidnapped Patti on January 4th, 1996, and videoed her as he raped her.

The Christmas gift photo of the makeup bag fouled Erick's plan. The makeup bag was visible in the sex videos Javedon recorded on January 4th -6th 1996 for the purpose of getting an acquittal on his trial for confine, battery and rape on October 26th – 30th, 1995. His planned to present the sex video and claim it was consensual sex in his October 26-30, 1995, trial. The plan was fouled due to the timing of Christmas photo with the makeup bag as a gift.

Hancock County Prosecutor Gossett had proof that Javedon kidnapped Patti on January 4th-6th, 1996, he charged Erick William Javedon with two kidnapping charges.

Detective Munden's evidence was proof that Erick had kidnapped Patti on January 4th, 1996, from her home to make a sex video with Patti wearing handcuffs. Javedon had planned to use the video in his trial to say Patti was willing to be handcuffed for sex in October. Prosecutor Larry Gossett charged Erick with kidnapping and rape.

This trial would be one of the most significant trials in Hancock County. Prosecutor Gossett prepared the case and sent for the evidence of thirty-eight video tapes. Detective Munden went to the Hancock County Jail Evidence Room to get the evidence for the trial. There were no videos in the evidence room. Hancock County Judge Snow had destroyed all videos. Or so they say they were destroyed, but at least one HCS deputy said he had one.

No Evidence! No trial. No justice for the victim.

Erick had committed numerous flagrant violations on other women, but he had never been brought to justice. The Pattern and history of Erick's unlawful but unprosecuted behavior demonstrated a criminal level of culpability that was being allowed to go on in Hancock County.

And yes, Erick had help. The people who helped Erick were aiding him, inducing injury-, and causing distress. In May 1992, Erick and hired men vandalized Patti's home causing damages of $3000.

Erick hired men to stalk her at the Indiana Government Center and follow her to the Julian center where she stayed.

On January 4th, 1996, one man helped Erick kidnap Patti. HCSD law enforcers had the sex videotapes of Eric as he raped Patti.

Erick was protected and free, and he bragged about it, and this was partly due to those who assisted him and turned a blind eye to his activities. They were and are as guilty as Erick!

Patti hoped for maximum punishment to protect other women and herself, but no one else seemed to hold this hope.

22

PROSECUTOR SEEKS REVIEW OF MISSING EVIDENCE

The headline of the *Greenfield Daily Reporter* read, "Hancock County Prosecutor Larry Gossett Requested a Special Prosecutor."

Judge Denies Review Of Missing Evidence

Judge Clovart denied Prosecutor Gossett's request to review the missing trial evidence. So, one can only think, "Why were the evidence tapes destroyed?" It was clear someone did not want Erick on trial.

Judge Freed Jevadon

In March 2006, officials submitted the evidence surrounding the case was destroyed. Because of missing trial evidence, Erick William Javedon walked out of the Hancock County court room free that day.

Although Erick received an eight-year sentence with two years to be served in prison, he walked out free that day with credit for time served; he was released and served the balance of the sentence on probation.

Judge Clovart handed down a plea bargain to a battery charge resulting in serious bodily injury, a Class C felony and FREED JEVADON that day.

Sadly, with Judge Clovart's ruling to deny the inquiry into the missing videotape evidence, "Truth and Justice" did not prevail for Patti.

Because of missing trial evidence, Erick William Javedon walked out of the Hancock County court room free that day. Although Erick received an eight-year sentence with two years to be served in prison, he walked out free that day with credit for time served; he was released and served the balance of the sentence on probation.

After every evil violation she had experienced from him, Patti and her family and friends in Hancock County were shocked that Erick was set free to walk out that day.

In the end, God has used Patti to share her story of His love and protection, so others will know they are not alone. It is her mission to give God the Glory for his love and care through the tortuous times. God was there with her, He is good!

> It is good for me that I have been afflicted; that I might learn thy statutes" (Psalm 119:71).

Patti has kept Detective John Munden's card since he started Investigating Erick William Javedon.

Since 1908   Greenfield, Indiana

Kidnap suspect freed after evidence is lost

Missing tapes force prosecutor into plea

Patricia Hinds Robinson, who now is a state employee, would have been a key witness in the case against William Hand Gevedon. Now, however, she won't be able to testify. Prosecutors made a deal with Gevedon after some videotapes that were to be used as evidence disappeared.

Tom Russo /
Daily Reporter

tence – two years in prison and six years on probation. He was released Friday with credit for time served. Gevedon's sentence was much lighter than expected since he had been

going to take Gevedon to trial and that a plea agreement was "highly unlikely."
That changed with the lost evidence,

because the prosecutor at the said he was not going to try t

See KIDNAP, ?

Accuser dismayed over deal

'He really is an evil person,' former girlfriend says

IN THE END............. "Truth and Justice" did not prevail for Patti.

Prayers and Promises

Patti often wondered why she lived through the years of evil attacks on her life, but she found God had a plan for her. She was amazed that God loved her so much that He would shelter her when she was repeatedly endangered. Patti was a Christian but did not serve God as she knew she should. That is why He chastised her to redirect her focus upon Him.

Why did she live? Because God used the circumstance:

- to teach her how much He loved her.

- to teach her how to trust Him.

- to be an agent of His peace.

- to teach her to have faith in Him.

- to share her story so others would know they are not alone.

- to break and change the stigma related to domestic violence.

- to work with Judge Jeanne Hamilton, Senator Breaux, and Sheriff Nick Gulling to get the $100 protective order fee dropped for domestic violence victims.

The Prayer of Patti's Heart:

Lord, help me to be a witness to Your saving grace in my life. Give me the blessings to communicate my story.

Oh God, help me today. I am ready to deliver the truth of a time in my life when You alone brought me through the most horrifying experiences.

Lord, I saw how You answered prayers and performed miracles. You surrounded me with Angels-KJV-4. You gave me strength. You taught me to depend on You and not to be afraid. You gave me *peace*!

Lord, I can now be glad I had these experiences because they taught me to believe in You and have *faith*.

Lord, help me to share my testimony that I may speak just what You want me to say for the Your glory.

In my stressful times, I called upon you, Lord, and found my almighty God is a Spirit who answers my needs. Father, thank you for being there. Thank you for your *love* and *protection* for all my family and me during this horrifying time in my life.

Amen.

The Promises of God

Patti leaned on many Bible verses during her ordeal. She relied on the principles of the Word of God and of living a Christian life. These are some verses and principles that sustained her.

> *Even the spirit of truth; whom the world cannot receive, because it seeth him not, neither knoweth him: but ye know him; for he dwelleth with you, and shall be in you (John 14:17).*

> *If ye shall ask anything in my name, I will do it (John 14:14).*

> *I will not leave you, comfortless: I will come to you (John 14:18).*

> *Peace I leave with you, my peace I give unto you: not as the world giveth. Let not your heart be troubled, neither let it be afraid (John 14:27).*

Therefore, if anyone is in Christ, the new creation has come: The old has gone, the new is here (II Corinthians 5:17).

David was greatly distressed; for the people spoke of stoning him . . . But David encouraged himself in the Lord his God. God is greater than the problem (Samuel 30:6).

Draw nigh to God, and He will draw nigh to you (James 4:8).

Thy word is a lamp unto my feet and a light unto my path (Psalm 119:105).

Trust in the Lord with all thine heart, and lean not unto thine understanding. In all ways acknowledge him, and He shall direct thy paths (Proverbs 3:5–6).

I will not fail thee, nor forsake thee (Joshua 1:5).

Unto thee, O LORD, do I lift up my soul O my God, I trust in thee: let me not be ashamed (Psalm 25:1–2).

Be merciful to me, my God, for my enemies are in hot pursuit; all day long they press their attack. My adversaries pursue me all day long; in their pride, many are attacking me. When I am afraid, I put my trust in you. In God, whose word I praise in God I trust and am not afraid. What can mere mortals do to me? (Psalm 56:1–4).

These Principles of Faith Trust God to Do All Things Well!

- Saved people have a relationship as a child of God.

- The Holy Spirit gives the wisdom to follow God's plan— *"He will guide you" (John 16:13).*

- Christians can become vessels for the Spirit of God— *"God can use us." (Ephesians 2:10).*

- Christians can see and appreciate supernatural things— *"Angels-4 and visions not visible to others" (II Corinthians 4:18)*-KJV.

God already knew Patti needed to learn basic principles of His love, to have faith, and to trust Him. Patti needed to believe in God's love for her. Now, Patti will never doubt how real His love is. She has learned God had an abundance of love for her. Patti was going along in her life when God put suffering in her life for a reason.

God knew she needed to grow in trust and faith in Him.

- Believe in God's care for you. He made provisions for her by revealing Himself to help her. That's when she learned to have faith and trust in God.

- Believe in God's commands. His righteousness shall come to you.

- God wants you to have trust and faith. Patti trusted God *would* protect her and grew strong with faith. With amazement, Patti believed that she was the specific person to whom God was showing His love and protection, and she learned to have absolute confidence and trust each day. God was with her in so many ways. Patti learned that God loves her so much.

- God protected Patti when she could not get help from anyone. Patti could not comprehend the depth of His love and protection.

- Pati has learned that fear and faith are mortal enemies. Faith was all Patti had, but *faith* was all Patti needed.

- Through telling her story, Patti wants every victim of abuse to know that God has abundant love for all.

With faith, our deepest needs can be heard, and then we can experience the success of faith in seeing God accomplish what is humanly impossible. Faith will magnify the Savior's Word, and faith will overcome the opposing forces of Satan and the evil he does in the world."

Faith brings peace.

God was with Patti like Daniel in the Lion's den.

Even amid terror, Patti found the sure wall of faith, and it was her faith that gave her peace. Faith brings power because faith is placed in a great Father who can do all things.

With faith comes grace—God gave Patti grace to turn her scars into stars. That Patti could find the power of faith in the middle of brutality was a beautiful thing. It was beautiful to know that the Almighty God was there with her in the center of her greatest struggle.

Faith flourished by showing itself in the conquest.

Faith is the convincing proof of unseen things . . . the evidence of things not seen. It is the spiritual sense through which the soul comes into contact with and is affected by the spiritual world.

What Is Domestic Violence[16]

Domestic violence (also known as domestic abuse, family violence, or intimate partner violence) occurs when a family member, partner, or ex-partner attempts to physically or psychologically dominate another.

114

Domestic violence-1 has many forms, including physical violence, sexual abuse, emotional abuse, intimidation, isolation, economic deprivation, and threats of violence. Violence can be criminal and includes physical assault (hitting, pushing, shoving, etc.), sexual abuse (unwanted or forced sexual activity), and stalking. Although emotional, psychological, and financial abuse is not criminal behavior in some legal systems, it is a form of abuse that can lead to criminal violence.

There are processes and resources to help those in an abusive or violent situation.

More is being done for victims. Victim assistance units are coordinating to end domestic and sexual violence. Over ten million people are victims of domestic and sexual violence each year.

Below are resources for those stuck in the Pattern and cycle of domestic violence.

Patti hopes these resources will help individuals identify the warning signs of domestic abuse and gain the tools they need to break the Pattern and cycle of abuse.

The cycle of violence in domestic abuse[17]

Domestic abuse falls into a common Pattern or cycle of violence:

Abuse – Your abusive partner lashes out with aggressive, belittling, or violent behavior. This treatment is a power play designed to show you "who is boss."

Guilt – Your partner feels guilt after abusing you but not because of their actions. They're more worried about being caught and facing the consequences of their abusive behavior.

Excuses – Your abuser rationalizes what they have done. The person may come up with a string of excuses or blame you for provoking them—anything to avoid taking responsibility.

"Normal" behavior – Your partner does everything in their power to regain control and ensure that you'll stay in the relationship. A perpetrator may act as if nothing has happened, or they might "turn on the charm." This peaceful honeymoon phase may give you hope that the abuser has changed this time.

Fantasy and planning – Your abuser begins to fantasize about repeating the abuse. They spend a lot of time thinking about what you've done wrong and how they'll make you pay for it. Then they form a plan for turning the fantasy of abuse into reality.

Set-up – Your abuser sets you up and puts their plan in motion, creating a situation where they can justify abusing you.

Your abuser's apologies and loving gestures in between the episodes of abuse can make it difficult to leave. They may cause you to believe that you are the only person who can help them, that they will change their behavior, and that they truly love you. However, the dangers of staying are very real.

The full cycle of domestic violence: An example of the Pattern

- A man **abuses** his partner. After he hits her, he experiences self-directed guilt. He says, "I'm sorry for hurting you." What he does not say is, "Because I might get caught."

- He then **rationalizes** his behavior by accusing his partner of having an affair. He tells her, "If you weren't such a worthless whore, I wouldn't have to hit you."

- He then **acts contrite**, reassuring her that it will not happen again.

- But later he **fantasizes** and reflects on past abuse and decides to hurt her again.

He **plans** on sending her to the grocery store, purposely choosing a busy time. She is then held up in traffic and returns a few minutes later than expected. In his mind, he justifies assaulting her by blaming her for having an affair with the store clerk. He has just **set her up**.

It's impossible to know with certainty what goes on behind closed doors, but there are some telltale signs of emotional abuse and domestic violence. If you witness these warning signs of abuse in a friend, family member, or co-worker, you must take them very seriously.

People who are being abused may:

- seem afraid or anxious to please their partner.

- go along with everything their partner says and does.

- check in often with their partner to report where they are and what they're doing.

- receive frequent, harassing phone calls from their partner.

- talk about their partner's temper, jealousy, or possessiveness.

Warning signs of physical abuse

People who are being physically abused may:

- have frequent injuries, with the excuse of "accidents."

- frequently miss work, school, or social occasions, without explanation.

- dress in clothing designed to hide bruises or scars (for example, wearing long sleeves in the summer or sunglasses indoors).

Warning signs of isolation

People who are being isolated by their abuser may:

- be restricted from seeing family and friends.

- rarely go out in public without their partner.

- have limited access to money, credit cards, or the car.

Warning signs of psychological abuse

People who are being abused psychologically may:

- have very low self-esteem, even if they used to be confident.

- show significant personality changes (e.g., an outgoing person becomes withdrawn).

- be depressed, anxious, or suicidal.

Speak Up If You Suspect Domestic Violence or Abuse

If you suspect that someone you know is being abused, speak up! If you're hesitating—telling yourself that it's none of your business, you might be wrong, or that the person might not want to talk about it—keep in mind that expressing your concern will let the person know that you care and may even save their life.

Talk to the person privately, and let them know you're concerned. Point out the signs you've noticed that worry you. Tell the person you're there for them whenever they feel ready to talk. Reassure them that you'll keep whatever is said between the two of you, and let them know that you'll help in any way you can.

Do:	Don't:
Ask if something is wrong	Wait for the person to come to you
Express your concern	Blame or judge them
Listen and validate	Pressure them to act
Offer to help	Give advice
Support their decisions	Place conditions on your support

Authors: Melinda Smith, M.A., and Jeanne Segal, Ph.D.
http://www.helpguide.org/articles/abuse/domestic-violence-and-abuse.html

Justice for Victims of Domestic Violence

In 2005, deputy prosecutor Brent Eaton, started pursuing justice for Patti against William Erick Javedon on the charges of kidnapping, criminal confinement, and battery. The video evidence needed for trial was missing. A request was denied for a review of the missing evidence. There was no trial. The abuser/kidnapper was set free with two kidnapping charges.

The author, Pat E. Robinson became a fighter for domestic violence victims by testifying in the Indiana Senate for improved domestic violence laws. She has been a long standing member of the Indiana Coalition Against Domestic Violence (ICADV).

Currently, Robinson is a volunteer with the Hancock County Prosecutor Brent Eaton's SART (Sexual Assault Response Team). Chief Deputy Prosecutor Aimee Herring is spearheading the multi-disciplinary protocols and collaborative responses to sexual assaults. The goal of the Hancock County SART is to use a team approach to provide compassionate, comprehensive evidence collection, emotional support, information, assistance, and investigation after an assault has occurred.

SART is a county-wide twenty-eight member multidisciplinary partnership designed for a timely response with compassionate help for sexual assault victims and their families.

God has inspired Robinson to help domestic abuse victims become survivors. She found God had a purpose for all she went through.

> "It is good for me that I have been afflicted; that I might
> learn thy statutes." PSALM 119:71.

She is passionate with her opportunity to be a SART volunteer to help domestic abuse victims. She has authored "The Predator" to help the domestic abuse victim understand the abuser's pattern of cyclical behaviors that trap them mentally, physically, and psychologically – dismantling equality in the relation and making the victim feel undeserving of respect. All readers can learn the warning signs and can benefit from the domestic violence help resources included in "The Predator."

Epilogue

"Family togetherness, the greatest earthly accomplishment."

The works of "The Predator" has awakened the author's senses to the devastation within her family that is still smoldering from the violent atmosphere they were engulfed in as children. They grew up living with domestic violence and the impact of this experience has lasted into their adult life. The extreme contrast of their violent abusive father and the broken spirit of their submissive mother left them as children lost to reality. Patti and her siblings were unknown to love, peace, security, and happy carefree family togetherness.

The experience of living in domestic violence and the horrible beatings their mother endured contributed to roles they assumed as children that reined in their adult life exhibiting such behaviors as: a controller, an abuser, a caretaker, and a parent.

This journey of authoring her book has given her a desire to empower her family to recover with a deep connection and loving relationships.

Authoring her true story has been her most personal reward to know that not only beyond breaking away from domestic violence, but to recover from a harmful environment and replace life filled with more love, peace, security, compassion and happy carefree 'family togetherness is the greatest earthly accomplishment.'

"God's promise to Patti!" I am going to send an Angel in front of you, to guard you on your way and to bring you to the place that I have prepared (Exodus 23:10). -KJV

THE END

IMAGE GALLERY

PATTI FIRST MET ERICK 1984.

One winter day in blizzard conditions a snow removal man was called to remove the massive snow drifts and ice from Patti's driveway. She met him in the garage, thanked him, and wrote a check for payment. Every time it snowed, Pati's driveway was cleared of snow and ice that year, but not at her not request.

1992 ERIC CALLED FOR A DATE

Eight years after clearing ice and snow from Patti's driveway, Erick called and told her he had gotten a divorce and was single. He said he read in the newspaper about her divorce and asked her to meet him for coffee. From the beginning, he was such a charmer, and Patti was immediately very attracted to him.

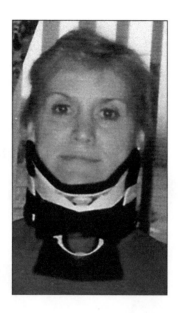

AFTER CAR ACCIDENT ABUSE BEGINS

Just one month after Patti started seeing Erick, she was involved in a head-on car accident suffering severe injuries to three cervical vertebrae. A two-year recovery period left her isolated. Behind Erick's façade of caring, attentive behavior, he soon worked his way deeper into Patti's life, where he would soon show his true colors.

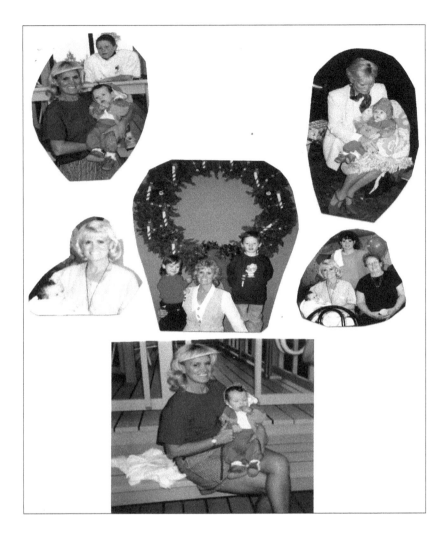

THREATS TO HER FAMILY

To control Patti, Erick threatens harm to Patti's mother Azalee, Patti's daughter Ramona, baby granddaughter Elizabeth, and her two grandsons, Justin the older, and Tyler the younger. She loved her family and did exactly what he wanted to keep them safe for she knew the evil he was capable of.

PATTI WITH DAUGHTER RAMONA

At Ramona and Rusty's wedding reception, Erick became jealous of Patti talking with friends.

Later he took his fury out on Patti at the lake.

PATTI'S DAUGHTER RAMONA AND SON GREG

Risked their lives in search of their mother.
THEY DID NOT GIVE UP THEIR SEARCH.

EVIDENCE FOR TWO KIDNAPPING CHARGES AGAINST ERICK

Detective John Munden had a photo of evidence with Patti unwrapping a make-up bag on Christmas Eve 1996. The make-up bag in the photo proves Javedon kidnapped Patti on January 4th-6th, 1996, and recorded the sex video after Christmas when he kidnapped Patti.

The identical make-up bag was visible in the sex videos HCSD confiscated at a hotel Javedon at been staying at when he eluded the sheriff and detectives. Then went on the run until the FBI caught him in Ohio.

Hancock County Prosecutor Gossett had charged Erick William Javedon on two charges of kidnapping. The trial date was set, however, when the prosecutor sent for the evidence, a video of the kidnapping and sexual assault had been destroyed by the judge. Over thirty sexual assault videos missing from the evidence room.

The prosecutor's request for an investigation was denied. There was no trial for the two kidnappings.

Erick William Javedon was set free.

There was no Justice for Patti. She and her family, friends and the community were devasted. Patti was unsafe again.

Patti was devastated.

No Justice!

Patti and Gary in their backyard.

In 2003, God sent my loving Christian husband, Gary into my life. He showers me with genuine love and companionship. His passion and support helped me in my long healing process as I wrote about the violence and relived it. His encouragement helped me write from my heart and soul. Thank you, my love!

Resources

- Hall, Scott. 1992. "Boyfriend charged in beating." *Daily Reporter,* July 15, 1992, A1.

- Helms, Janet. 1996. "Fugitive in Federal Custody." *Daily Reporter,* October 4, 1996, A1.

- Helms, Janet. 2005. "Prisoner will face $1 million bond." *Daily Reporter,* February 11, 2005, A1.

- Helms, Janet. 2005. "'I know society needs to help:' Woman speaks out to build a case against Gevedon." *Daily Reporter,* February 26, 2005, A1.

- Hodson, Janet. 2005. "Judge still needed for Gevedon trial." *Daily Reporter,* September 28, 2005, 1A.

- Moyer, Traci. 2006. "Kidnap suspect freed after evidence is lost: Missing tapes force prosecutor into plea." *Daily Reporter,* March 26, 2006, A1.

- News Staff. 1996. "THE TOP LOCAL STORIES OF 1996." *Daily Reporter,* December 31, 1996, A1.

- North, Eric. 2005. "Defendant seeks new judge: Request delays trial for man accused of 1990s kidnapping." *Daily Reporter,* September 21, 2005, 1A.

- North, Eric. 1995. "1 charged in beating." *Daily Reporter,* November 7, 1995, A1.

- North, Eric. 1995. "Fugitive faces new charges." *Daily Reporter,* November 15, 1995, A1.

- North, Eric. 1996. "Federal charges next in hunt for city fugitive." *Daily Reporter,* February 28, 1996, A1.

- North, Eric. 1999. "Gevedon guilty on 7 weapon charges." *Daily Reporter,* February 28, 1999, A1.

- Scott, Dave. 1996. "Search Intensifies for area fugitive: (thirty-eight pornographic rape videos)." *Daily Reporter,* February 2, 1996, A1.

- Staff Reports. 2005. "Gevedon brought back to Indiana Hancock county." *Daily Reporter,* May 18, 2005, A1.

- Stanton, Jeff. 1996. "Local man sought in confinement case." *Daily Reporter,* January 17, 1996, A1.

- Steele, Noelle M. 2006. "Lost tapes won't be investigated: Prosecutor: Judge ruling ends inquiry into destruction of Gevedon video." *Daily Reporter,* March 28, 2006, A1.

NOTES

1. The US Department of Justice defines domestic violence as "a pattern of abusive behavior in any relationship that is used by one partner to gain or maintain power and control over another intimate partner." Domestic violence can be verbal, physical, sexual, or psychological. Abusive people believe they have the right to control and restrict the lives of their partners, often either because they believe their own feelings and needs should be the priority in the relationship or because they enjoy exerting the power that such abuse gives them. There is a thin line between the terms "domestic violence" and "domestic abuse." Domestic violence and domestic abuse are two common terms that are typically used to describe various unlawful acts in a court of law.

2. "Devastatingly Pervasive: 1 in 3 Women Globally Experience Violence," World Health Organization, March 9, 2021, https://www.who.int/news/item/09-03-2021-devastatingly-pervasive-1-in-3-women-globally-experience-violence.

3. See endnote 1.

4. "The Pattern" in the full Cycle of Domestic Violence is a common pattern or cycle of abuse used by abusers. (Abuse n.d.)

5. See endnote 4.

6. Billy Graham, *Angels: God's Secret Agents* (Nashville, Tennessee: W Publishing Group, Thomas Nelson, Inc., 1975, 1986, 1994, 1995).

7. "Devastatingly Pervasive: 1 in 3 Women Globally Experience Violence," World Health Organization.

8. See endnote 4.

9. See endnote 4.

10. See endnote 4.

11. See endnote 4.

12. See endnote 4.

13. See endnote 4.

14. Firearms and Explosives Bureau of Alcohol, Tobacco, *Federal Firearms Regulations Reference Guide: ATP Pub 5300.4* (Washington, DC: 4th Watch Publishing Co., 2014).

15. Firearms and Explosives Bureau of Alcohol, Tobacco, *Federal Firearms Regulations Reference Guide: ATP Pub 5300.4.*

16. See endnote 1.

17. See endnote 4.

CPSIA information can be obtained
at www.ICGtesting.com
Printed in the USA
BVHW012230090323
660165BV00015B/106